THE CATAPULT EFFECT
13 PRINCIPLES OF WAR IN BUSINESS

Musekiwa Samuriwo

About the author

Musekiwa Samuriwo is an entrepreneur and business development consultant specialising in strategy, product development and futures research. He has eleven years of experience working in software development, branding and advertising and training and development. He has founded 3 technology companies, Cybercard Enterprise Solutions, OPEXA (Open Exchange Africa) and CQE. He is the author of 2 other books, The God Idea and The Shark and the Japanese Fisherman and an avid and broad reader. He holds a Master's In Business Administration from the University of Steinbeis in Germany.

First Edition

Originally published in English under the title "The Catapult Effect: 13 Principles of War in Business by Musekiwa Samuriwo in 2019

ISBN: 978-1-77906-582-7

DTP – African Knight Publishers

Consulting Editor – Selina Zigomo

TABLE OF CONTENTS

Shaping the Sputnik Moment

Hence the saying: If you know the enemy and know yourself, you need not fear the result of a hundred battles. If you know yourself but not the enemy, for every victory gained you will also suffer a defeat. If you know neither the enemy nor yourself, you will succumb in every battle.[1]

Sun Tzu

---

[1] Sun-Tzu Sunzi *The Art of War*, (Long river Press 2003),11

Chapter 1 DISCOVER YOUR SPUTNIK MOMENT.

It is no secret that the world is presently entering into a deepening and seemingly nebulous crisis. No one can really pinpoint or fully express the problems that oppose us. The globe's problems range from political, social, economic to environmental. Our problems are complex, extremely dynamic and volatile.

Just as nations plug one hole another one springs up. As a dedication to the crises and challenges the Japanese (especially the fishermen) have encountered over the past few years like earthquakes, a tsunami and nuclear disaster and the problems different people are facing all over the globe, I present this chapter.

It reflects my deepest conviction that society as a whole and entrepreneurs in different contexts though faced with seemingly insurmountable problems have the opportunity to dig deep and unlock the reserves of potential that result in what is commonly called the Sputnik Moment.

History is turning the corner and presents us with an environment brimming with paradoxes, volatility, and adaptive complexity. It is in this context; in the face of peril that I believe the Japanese fisherman will find significant opportunities to unlock sustainable value.

This time is for the entrepreneur and the business ready to take a step forward in spite of the ever-present difficulties and challenges. President Obama once hailed the information age as the all-new Sputnik Moment for America. I believe it is the Sputnik Moment for everyone who chooses to face their challenges head on with conviction and a single minded devotion in pursuit of success and significance.[2]

---

[2]   Barack   Obama,   *State   of   the   Union   Address* *https://www.theguardian.com/world/2011/jan/26/state-of-the-union-address-obama-sputnik-moment*

WHAT IS A SPUTNIK MOMENT?

The words 'sputnik moment' were first used as a reference to the Soviet Union satellite launched called the Sputnik 1, and beat the USA into space.[3]

> "A Sputnik moment is a trigger mechanism, an event that makes people collectively say that they need to do something, and this sets a course in another direction," [4]
>
> Roger Launius, National Air and Space Museum.

It is also the point where people realise that they are threatened or challenged and have to redouble their efforts to survive, catch up and grow.

WHAT IS THE NEXT GREAT LEAP FORWARD FOR YOUR BUSINESS AND LIFE?

This is a question we must all ask ourselves, in light of the reality and context we live in. It, therefore, goes without

---

[3]http://www.usingenglish.com/reference/idioms/sputnik+moment.

[4] https://www.space.com/10437-sputnik-moment.html

saying that to avoid answering this question is tantamount to failure. For the Japanese fisherman (entrepreneur), it is the inalienable question that determines growth, by defining how to maximise the endless waves of blue oceans waiting to be harnessed.

As an entrepreneur, you may have survived the onslaughts and diversionary tactics of sharks. You may have had moments where all hope seemed lost but, are now enjoying some semblance of success and victory, stagnation or temporary stability. It is at this point, that the question above must be answered.

In the following chapters, I will proceed to share principles I have come to call the Catapult Effect. I believe these principles are simple tools that a fisherman can apply to answer this critical question and take the great leap forward towards significance.

They are reflections that will help the entrepreneur discover their Sputnik Moment and trigger quantum growth.

The Catapult Effect will reveal how to:

I. Discover the right positioning to challenge for market share.

II. Harness the power of vision.

III. Maximize limited resources.

IV. How to convert some liabilities and toxic assets into well-oiled assets that create wealth.

V. Take significant steps forward like a well-trained army, and many other lessons.

The principles I call the Catapult Effect constitute steps an entrepreneur can take towards establishing a competitive and unassailable strategic position in the market place. These principles are designed for one objective - victory.

The Catapult Effect propounds that what an entrepreneur was unable to do before, is now possible with the help of an innovative throwing (growing) mechanism. Nothing is more imperative in these volatile times than the ability to survive in difficult circumstances and ultimately to find the space to thrive.

Sun Tzu teaches on the five essentials for victory:[5]

---

[5] Sun Tzu, *The Art of War: A New Translation,* (Amber Books 2012)

I. **He will win who knows when to fight and when not to fight:** The 13 principles outlined in this book help an entrepreneur choose battles wisely by investing in building a strong and sustainable business.

II. **He will win who knows how to handle both superior and inferior forces:** These principles teach an entrepreneur how to work with minimal resources as a master *strategoi*. Some of the greatest generals in history worked with inferior forces to attain victory by the use of strategy.

III. **He will win whose army is animated by the same spirit throughout all its ranks:** Motivation and inspiration are powerful drivers of success and victory. The best inspiration is derived from well implemented strategies and plans.

IV. **He will win who, prepared himself, waits to take the enemy unprepared:** The 13 principles help your business prepare for offensive action against a competitor by unlocking your unique abilities.

V. **He will win who has military capacity and is not interfered with by the sovereign**: Core to the success of a business is the role of leadership in inspiring action and minimizing administrative interference with operations.

STIMULATING YOUR BUSINESS AND YOUR LIFE.

Crises in whatever form they come serve as the seedbed for a prosperous future. It is a choice to either look at difficult situations or extenuating realities as the end of our rope or to look at them as the beginning of something altogether fresh and new. For the people of Japan who've faced daunting and seemingly insurmountable difficulties, it has been a moment to rediscover the treasure within the box, the realities outside the box and the boundless opportunities beyond. This also can be the case for entrepreneurs.

Dan Clark once said, "...all the answers to life can be found in the box."[6] I believe this to be true and would add that the answers are also just outside the box and some of the answers lie beyond the box. The Japanese fisherman (entrepreneur) must discover the latent potential resident within their brain and business, understand their current and emergent contexts and see what lies in the boundless beyond.

It is these discoveries that make the shark (competitor) irrelevant and pale, in the light of the immanent and emergent possibilities. Anyone who is able to bear adversity with the resolve to reach the light at the end of the tunnel like the Japanese and the people in my homeland Zimbabwe deserves the utmost respect. Entrepreneurs who can seize the moment, and take the great leap forward towards significance, by maximising their potential must be celebrated.

---

[6] Dan Clark, *The Art Of Significance*,(Penguin Publishing Group 2013)

"Japanese fishermen, my fellow entrepreneurs, this is the moment in history that we stand bold in spite of the current trials and challenges we face. We are resolute and firm in our bid to grow our businesses, transform our lives and influence our communities. Let it be said that we did not shrink back in the face of adversity or in the midst of sharks; great white and all.

Rather, let it be said that we discovered the potential within ourselves, embraced our volatile environment and shaped the future economy. Let it be said that we seized the day and stepped into our SPUTNIK MOMENT!"

The African Knight

Chapter 2 SHAPING THE SPUTNIK MOMENT

In my previous book *The Shark and the Japanese Fisherman*, [7] I discuss some pressing encumbrances entrepreneurs encounter when they sail the open seas of opportunity. There are four key dangers that expose the unwitting entrepreneur to the shark; desperation, naivety, ignorance and greed.

I propose that entrepreneurs can become Japanese fishermen, capable business people who are able to overcome sharks and fully maximise the potential of their business ideas. Furthermore, I explore how Japanese fishermen have the ability to go beyond competing for the same market share by creating market space through innovation, leveraging and collaboration.

In many ways the turbulent waters of hardship and uncertainty serve as a rallying cry to all entrepreneurs, to

---

[7] Musekiwa Samuriwo, *The Shark and The Japanese Fisherman*, African Knight 2013

pursue something greater. The future is for the taking and it's very possible that the small entrepreneur of today will be the market leader of tomorrow, simply because they finally grasped the principles laid down in this book called the *Catapult Effect*.

THE CATAPULT EFFECT #BUSINESSISWAR

> The good fighters of old first put themselves beyond the possibility of defeat, and then waited for an opportunity of defeating the enemy.[8]
>
> Sun Tzu

My amateur love for ancient history; Persian, Greek and Roman empires has given me a rich understanding of war and the rise and fall of kingdoms. It is through the many lessons from historical icons such as Jesus, Sun Tzu and many others that the 13 principles of war have been expounded in this book.

Accordingly, I've come to name these principles after a weapon that I believe changed the face of war in ancient

---

[8] Sun Tzu *The Art of War*, 10

times; especially when advancing armies besieged a city. The catapult (*onager* / *mangonell*) was a weapon designed to break down a city's walls from a greater distance, with more force and power than the bow, so as to open up opportunities (weaknesses) to advance and take over the city.

The Catapult Effect is a combination of 13 unique principles of war that can change the course of any business. Faced with sharks of varying sizes and enemies (competitors) with different strategies, it is imperative that the fisherman learn and apply these key principles to shape and develop their sputnik moment; which is the next critical phase of growth in business. In the next few chapters, I will proceed to fully expound on the principles below,

I.   A Secure base
II.   Strategic thinking
III. Visioning and goal setting
IV.   Sustaining the vision and goal
V.   Initiating offensive action
VI.   Concentration of forces

VII.   Economy of forces

VIII.   Stealth attacks

IX.   Mobility and flexibility (effective and efficient decision making)

X.   The power of cooperation (power of team and collaboration)

XI.   Security (protecting secured positions and markets)

XII.   The principle of pursuit (going for it)

XIII. Forming public opinion (building brand equity)

It is important to develop and maintain a sustainable competitive advantage for the express reason that it ensures that a business has a viable future and is protected against the threat of voracious sharks. Conversely, the Japanese fisherman must ensure the business can survive and grow significantly in spite of various challenges and threats.

Being an entrepreneur in Zimbabwe I have grown to appreciate these principles as they have thrust me more effectively towards my desired and intended future. I have seen the significance of building from a secure position, working with a strategy and the power of vision.

Most important of these is the ability to choose one's battles wisely in spite of 'limited' resources or indefensible market positions.

Over the next few chapters, it is my express intention and goal to inspire entrepreneurs - Japanese fishermen, to move from strength to strength using the *Catapult Effect*. This will in turn shape 'sputnik moments' and establish successful, sustainable businesses that add value and create wealth.

There is no obstacle that can hinder the progress of a Japanese fisherman. Thomas Carlyle puts it this way, "The block of granite which was an obstacle in the pathway of the weak, became a stepping-stone in the pathway of the strong."[9] The world will celebrate the entrepreneur who chooses to blaze a path worthy of remembrance as the man called Pericles an Ancient Greek leader who is considered the father of modern day democracy.

---

[9] Geri O'Neill, *Make The Best Of The Rest Of Your Life* (DoctorZed Publishing 2010), 71

"Future ages will wonder at us, as present ages wonder at us now." [10]

Pericles 460 B.C.

Our choice must be to be remembered in the future as entrepreneurs who endeavoured to unlock and create lasting value.

---

[10] James I Porter, *Classical Pasts: The Classical Traditions of Greece and Rome* (Princeton University Press, 2006), 62

Chapter 3 BUILDING FROM A SECURE BASE – *THE CASTRA*

One of the most important things in any given strategic campaign, military or otherwise, which is often disregarded, is the base camp or launch position. To the layman the military base seems to contribute very little to the offensive action. Similarly, in business, certain things are not considered as important when an entrepreneur looks to launch their business.

A secure base is the foundation of building a business that will stand the test of time. It must therefore be understood that even though from a superficial view, something may not seem to add value to the overall offensive campaign to launch a product, does not mean that it is not important.

This principle does not propound that an entrepreneur set up an elaborate corner office, though having a place to operate from is important. Rather it is a principle that has seven key dimensions that contribute to the development of a lasting business. Many entrepreneurs have started their businesses in dingy garages, kitchens, bedrooms and so forth. Where you start is of little consequence.

Establishing a lasting business is not so much about the geographical location as it is about building on this critical foundation. It is the activities and thought processes you engage in to seize the future that matters. These are intangible activities necessary to ensure that a business takes off on the right footing.

The secret to Roman conquest was their ability to build a secure base in any location. The Romans were masters of the siege and always built a secure base close enough to the besieged city to attack but far enough to be safe from enemy assaults. Most siege works and supporting weaponry like the *onager* were built on the spot.[11] From this we learn that an entrepreneur can build a secure base anywhere, it all really comes down to mindset and drive.

---

[11] *Onager* is an ancient Roman torsion-powered weapon similar to a catapult. Accessed 10 December 2018. www.britannica.com

SEVEN DIMENSIONS OF A SECURE BASE,

I.   Planning
II.   Training and Equipping
III.   Reserves
IV.   Brand Identity
V.   Know-how and Skill
VI.   A resting place
VII.   Launchpad (positioning)

PLANNING

Every great military campaign was initiated by paying great and meticulous attention to the details of the battle and war. The hallmark of great generals and warriors was often evident in the base before it was revealed on the battlefields. Entrepreneurs for all intents and purposes must have a quiet place – a base from which to contemplate and plan. When an entrepreneur plans and discusses tactics amid the noise of battle, it most likely turns out disastrously wrong.

Yet, this is often what entrepreneurs do particularly in Zimbabwe. We rush off into battle without considering all the permutations and aspects of the industry and the powerful incumbent holding market share. Planning is an imperative aspect of war and business. I would argue that 65% of a battle is fought over maps to resource and position men for battle, 30% of a battle is down to the skill, morale and motivation of the men and 5% is the fighting itself. Without comprehensive and detailed planning it is most likely that any engagement with the enemy will result in failure, no matter how skilled and equipped the army is.

Five knows of planning

I. **Know Yourself**: It is imperative to assess and be aware of your capabilities and shortcomings. To know yourself implies a degree of self-awareness that serves as a spur to advance your ideas. A business that lacks self-awareness most certainly lacks identity. Ignorance of one's potentialities and capabilities beckons disaster, and always leads to defeat.

II. **Know The Customer**: Understand the needs of the customer. The assumption that every conquered tribe ascribed and subscribed to *Pax Romana* or Roman peace was the demise of the Roman Empire. An awareness of the customer is crucial

24

before any offensive action is initiated. The famous warrior queen of the British Celtic Iceni Tribe Boudicca once rose against the Romans in AD 61 by attacking the Roman colony of Camulodunum (Colchester). [12] The rebellion was successful because the Romans ill-treated the inhabitants of the city. Thus when Boudicca attacked, the residents of the city turned against the Romans.

III. **Know Your Enemy:** An entrepreneur must know the competition and their capacity. Entrepreneurs often assume that the enemy is weaker and unable to handle their innovative approach to their market. The key operative word here is assumption. A key ingredient for the success of any military campaign is to acknowledge and respect the enemy. When generals and great leaders made assumptions about the enemy they were often proven to be fatally wrong. Untested and

---

[12] Nic Fields, *Boudicca's Rebellion AD 60–61: The Britons rise up against Rome,* (Bloomsbury USA 2011)

unfettered assumptions are dangerous and eat away at potential success.

IV. **Know The Terrain/Industry:** Develop a keen and curious awareness of the industry you're operating in and the potential industries you may disrupt. The mark of a true entrepreneur is the ability to recognize an opportunity. This is not a mere knowledge of the customer but an understanding of the technologies and tools available to effectively deliver a solution. An entrepreneur must have a keen and fond interest in the industry and terrain they intend to engage.   This is the core purpose of the process of mapping. It is critical to understand the ideal routes to take in order to achieve the object of the campaign - victory.

V. **Know The Environment:** Have an appreciation of the context and conditions of the world you're operating in. Beyond the industry lies a macro-environment shaped by climatic conditions, the sways and trappings of politics, the shrewd exchange of money and the often fickle interactions of a community. Planning for certain conditions serves to prepare the entrepreneur for success.

TRAINING AND EQUIPMENT

An entrepreneur in business must assume a position and area where they can learn and develop the necessary capacity and acumen to implement their business idea profitably. In the military, a secure base represents a place or an area dedicated for training and development and for storing equipment like ordnances. The necessary theory and facts are developed and tested in the base to ensure victory once the decision to attack a specific market has been made.

> The good fighters of old first put themselves
> beyond the possibility of defeat, and then waited
> for an opportunity of defeating the enemy. [13]
>
> Sun Tzu

As with the great generals of old, entrepreneurs must position themselves to be convinced beyond reasonable doubt that their business idea is a winner. This comes from

---

[13] Giles, *Sun Tzu On The Art Of War*, (Routledge 2005), 26

gathering the right information and simulating the business. Before committing any resources to implementation, like a good fighter the entrepreneur must practice and train. The war is not won on the battlefield; it is won in the training field through good preparation.

In war, training is both in combat and strategies. The very concepts of scenario planning and simulations have their origins in the tent of a general. To win battles and subsequently the war is determined by effectively creating as many scenarios as feasibly possible. Often this can negatively be viewed as paralysis by analysis but Sun Tzu captures the essence of good planning; the act of making the relevant and necessary calculations for victory.

The Spartans had a training philosophy called *Agoge* which focused on developing a strong individual. It involved both, combat and non-combat activities such as learning stealth, cultivating loyalty to the Spartan group, military training, hunting, dancing, singing and social interaction. [14] This combination of activities was designed to make the Spartans a cohesive fighting force and social unit.

> Now the general who wins a battle makes many calculations in his temple where the battle is fought. The general who loses a battle makes but few calculations beforehand. Thus do many calculations lead to victory, and few calculations to defeat: how much more no calculation at all! It is by attention to this point that I can foresee who is likely to win or lose. [15]
>
> Sun Tzu

A secure base is also a place where weapons and the necessary equipment for war and business must be stored. The armoury of weapons or cache is critical in battle. This may represent the ideas and plans of a business. Ideas should never be regarded as fickle, as they form the seedbed of successful businesses.

---

[14] Linda D. Coker, *Larentina: Myth, Legend, Legacy* (iUniverse 2011) 28

[15] Sun Tzu *The Art of War*, 3

Without ideas, concepts and solutions to problems it is likely there would be no business at all. One may be financially armed but without a problem to solve, an idea to execute and an armoury of solutions to implement, it can be said there is no business. Nonetheless it is not the mere store of ideas that makes a good business; it is their viability.

A cache of weapons that work in battle is vital. In ancient times, one of the most important roles in war was that of the blacksmith. The blacksmiths worked tirelessly sharpening dulled blades in the base, to ensure that theirs were the best swords possible to win a war. The Greeks won their battles because of the quality of their bronze weaponry which was well maintained. Similarly as a result of the superior quality of their iron artillery which was prepared and stored at a secure base, the Romans through conquest built their empire.

The concept of the game changer.

Dr Strive Masyiwa in a blog article once mentioned that he never goes into business without having a game changer.[16] This forms the crux of the *Catapult Effect* and is inferred in the importance of having an armoury. What shifts the tide of a battle is an army well-endowed with a good supply of the right weapons; in the case of a business the right information combined with the right ideas, unleashed at the right time serve as a game changer. This can also be a well-designed innovation that can change the face of the battle and guarantee success.

The *onager* and *corvus* were great military innovations that changed the course of war in ancient times. Consider that these were developed in quiet and secluded places within a secure base. These innovative weapons were at some point ideas drawn on paper. Yet, eventually they became three dimensional game changing tools that represented a deep seated desire for victory.

---

[16] Dr Strive Masiyiwa, accessed 10 December 2018. https://www.facebook.com/strivemasiyiwa/photos/learn-to-find-the-game-changer.

RESERVES

An army at battle requires reserves and supplies of different resources, as does an emerging business. A good general understands that a campaign, may take longer than anticipated and must be prepared for the unexpected. I once started a business with a colleague on the premise that we had designed a good product that would create value for our clients. However it became apparent that things were going to take longer than anticipated when we launched into the market.

> Thus, though we have heard of stupid haste in war, cleverness has never been seen associated with long delays. [17]
>
> Sun Tzu

This could have been the downfall of the business had there not been stores of critical reserves in the form of passion and cash-flow. Reserves can be anything from, human resources, working capital to intangible qualities such as drive and determination that buffer an entrepreneur in the midst of unanticipated setbacks.

---

[17] Giles, *Sun Tzu On The Art of War*, 11

Delays in implementation or sudden changes in the environment without available reserves, has left many an entrepreneur exposed to the perils of failure and disappointment in business.

> It is only one who is thoroughly acquainted with the evils of war that can thoroughly understand the profitable way of carrying it on. [18]
>
> Sun Tzu

It is one who is thoroughly acquainted with the evils of business who will appreciate the need for backup and counter plans in tow, with the required resources in reserve to execute them.

Recently I was involved in a project where there was no appreciation or provision made for the effect of delays on the outcome of the project. Worse still there were no back up plans or strategic reserves to mitigate such delays. The result was near catastrophic. This experience quickly brought to mind the significance of setting aside strategic

---

[18] Giles, *Sun Tzu On The Art Of War*, 12

reserves for any delay and the importance of avoiding them altogether.

BRAND IDENTITY

One of the most important things about an army is its identity or reputation. In offensive action, a certain portion of the battle is won on the basis of the army's reputation. An entrepreneur must consider reputation and identity as something very critical. Brand Identity, is a combination of different elements that help an entrepreneur launch a strong business. There are certain elements that an entrepreneur needs to look at and consider:

- **Brand Name:** what you will be called.
- **Logo and symbol**: how you will be identified.
- **Characters**: how you will be understood.
- **Slogans**: what people should expect.
- **Packaging**: how it will be presented.

If you look at an army, these elements can significantly determine the outcome of a battle. Ancient war general Genghis Khan's army was well known for its ruthlessness and that he often marched into an empty village. [19] The elements above built his reputation and determined how his enemies (competitors) perceived him.

KNOW HOW AND SKILL (COMPETENCE)

Launching from a secure base requires the necessary skills and competencies to launch a campaign. The lack thereof results in failure or defeat.

An entrepreneur must build a certain degree of skills and know-how relevant to the business they are entering into. Skill is a key ingredient in giving an entrepreneur confidence and courage to challenge for market share in a given competitive environment. This is how the Romans emerged as a force to be reckoned with from among other strong nations.

Rome was surrounded by great warring nations, like the Persians, Macedonians, Greeks and Phoenicians, who all had key competencies that made them strong fighting nations. The Phoenicians were great seamen, the Macedonians were known for their impenetrable phalanx,

---

[19] Mark Grossman, *World Military Leaders: A Bibliographical Dictionary*,(Infobase Publishing 2007) 126

the Persians relied on their sheer force of numbers and the Carthaginians were specialists in strategy.

The Romans emerged as a professional, aggressive and organised close combat force with small iron swords and large shields. And to succeed amongst strong competitors they had to be different and have a superior approach[20]. An entrepreneur must develop their skills and abilities that differentiate them from the competition. It is these skills developed in a secure environment that determine the success of a campaign.

RESTING PLACE

A secure base represents a place where an army can rest and recuperate to regain momentum and strength for the next onslaught.   The one thing that plagues most entrepreneurs is the lack of rest and reflection. Entrepreneurs are generally always on the advance and attack, proverbially called the hustle. They often lack the critical time to reset and reflect on key areas of their business.

---

[20] Malik, F., 2016. Strategy: Navigating the Complexity of the New World (Vol. 3). Campus Verlag

From pushing their product, to networking, most entrepreneurs are generally always on the move. More often than not entrepreneurs do not rest and review their strategic direction. An army that does not rest or have a place to convalesce will ultimately experience fatigue, which eventually leads to defeat. Rest means finding a context and environment where an entrepreneur can be reinvigorated after a defeat. A secure base represents a place or context where a leader can maintain the morale of his troops.

POSITIONING (LAUNCH PAD)

The Romans were reputed to travel with all the tools and resources necessary to besiege a city. This included carpenters, blacksmiths and so forth with all their tools. They would always be ready to establish a base of operations and position themselves for battle.

A secure base serves as a firm place to launch a campaign. From launching a product in a small niche retail outlet, obscure from the large manufacturer's turf, to creating open source software among fellow techies; it is important that an entrepreneur establish the optimal platform to launch their business.

To be positioned correctly is imperative for the survival of a business. Positioning implies that a business must be placed strategically enough to have a wide ranging view of the environment. History shows us that battles were fought in valleys but I believe they were won in the mountains.

During the Second World War, there was a Japanese general who eyed the location for his base in South East Asia. It was a cliff that gave him a panoramic view of the battleground and surrounding areas.

The battles may have been fought in the valleys below but the important thing was that the general had a secure base that gave him a clear view of his surroundings. This allowed him to plan and determine the ideal positions to initiate attacks. A more recent example many will recall, is the technique that the Zimbabwe National Army (ZNA) employed to take control of Zimbabwe in November 2017.

The ZNA had secure and strategic bases located across the country which gave them an advantage to initiate a smooth and first-of-its-kind political transition. Civilians and politicians alike were surprised at the sight of tanks being deployed from their barracks. It was swift, unexpected and effective which can all be attributed to having secure bases.

Indicators of a good Launchpad

The Market's Attractiveness

  i.   Is there a large market for the product or solution?
  ii. How fast is the market growing?
  iii. Is the competition weak or strong?
  iv. Does the industry have strong or high barriers to entry?
  v.   Is the industry prone to shocks and downturns during tough economic cycles?

The Entrepreneur's positioning

  i.   Is there potential for good market share?
  ii. Does your product or solution deliver equivalent or superior quality and value?
  iii. Do you have a strong and protectable brand, product or solution?

iv.   Are the costs to deliver product low with the potential to generate high profits?

Armed with these elements and having established a secure base from which to launch from, an entrepreneur is ready to consider the next important principle – Strategic Thinking.

Chapter 4 THE STRATEGOI (THE GENERALS) – THE ABILITY TO THINK AND ESTABLISH STRATEGY

In war, then, let your great object be victory, not lengthy campaigns. [21]

Sun Tzu

In this modern era it is becoming increasingly difficult to predict the future due to increasing and unrelenting volatility. Strategy becomes a vital tool to ensure businesses develop and grow towards sustained profitability. It is not impressive marketing campaigns or products that we should pursue as an end goal but the ability to consistently deliver value to the customer for a profit. The word strategy is derived from the Greek word *strategos* which is a military term translated to mean the general of an army.[22]

---

[21] Giles, *Sun Tzu On The Art Of War*, 12
[22] Azhdar Karami, *Strategy Formulation in Entrepreneurial Firms* (Ashgate Publishing Ltd 2007), 3

Strategy can be defined using the following terms,

- **A plan**: Something contrived at inception of an endeavour and monitored from start to end to ensure success.
- **A ploy**: A short term position, with limited objectives which can be altered at the shortest notice. It has a limited number of objectives that can easily be changed. Ploys are used in war as a threat or provocation to elicit a particular response.
- **A perception**: Strategy is also a way of viewing the world or a particular situation. Much like a worldview such as *Pax Romana* was a perception that drove the Roman Empire.
- **A pattern of behaviour**: Consistent and habitual action towards an intended outcome such as the actions of the Greeks under Alexander the Great.
- **A competitive position**: Strategy is also your position in light of or in contrast to your competitors.

Thinking strategically means adapting to the future or maintaining a safe position in the game until the dust clears. This chapter focuses on providing insight into the importance of thinking strategically and the ability to establish a strategy that can effectively create the necessary momentum for growth. Thinking strategically means basing business actions on the anticipated reaction that could result from the said action and not necessarily on theory, principles or general laws of practice.

There are 3 strategies for the entrepreneur seeking to establish a business in an existing market. These are: creating a niche, reconfiguring the value chain and leveraging (the very essence of the catapult effect).

FOUR DIMENSIONS OF STRATEGIC THOUGHT

It is imperative that an entrepreneur consider and plan a course of action necessary to establish and grow their business. To think strategically an entrepreneur must:

I.   Combine analytical skills with the ability to synthesize different elements and patterns i.e. combining creative and critical thinking.

II. Be visual and verbal in the appreciation of your business and the environment.

III. Be insightful. See what is clear and explicit as well as what is hidden and implied.

IV. Combine the passion in the heart with the logic in the mind. I often say the longest distance one must travel is between their heart and their mind.

These dimensions of strategic thought make it possible for an entrepreneur to see a situation or opportunity for what it really is, thereby positioning them to create the necessary plan to maximise the emergent opportunity or problem.

They were the ingredients that made some of the most celebrated generals in history great. For instance the Romans who defeated the Phoenicians using a peculiar innovation at sea, Hannibal of Carthage who endeavoured to conquer Rome and Alexander the Great who sought to conquer the known world including the mighty Persian Empire.

Thinking though necessary is not sufficient. It follows logic as with the example of the great generals above, that once there is clarity of thought; clarity of action must ensue.

Therefore it is important to establish a strategy that propels the business to the next level. The Phoenicians were renowned sailors whilst the Romans were reputed land combatants. This made for interesting confrontations. For the Romans to overcome the Phoenicians at sea, they had to leverage on their strengths to compensate for their seafaring weaknesses.

History records that the Roman army built a boarding bridge called the *corvus* which enabled the Romans to board enemy ships. This innovation gave them a great advantage. The thought and intent behind the *corvus* was to take their land combat skills to sea. The result was the development of a bridge that aided Roman soldiers' board enemy ships, to engage in close combat.[23]

AN ENTREPRENEUR'S CORVUS

Similarly, an entrepreneur must consider the internal strength of their business and formulate a means to counter the strength of the incumbent competitor. In

---

[23] Brian Todd Carey, Joshua Allfree, John Cairns, *Warfare In The Ancient World* (Pen and Sword)

essence, every entrepreneur must develop a *corvus*, a tool that translates internal strengths to effective market development and penetration. The following strategies should be considered singly or as combinations to implement and secure a competitive advantage in the market place.

NICHE – CREATING A SPECIALIZED AND PROFITABLE CORNER OF THE MARKET

By finding a specific target audience that is not fully satisfied by the existing services available in the market, an entrepreneur can optimise their competitive advantage. Using a core strength or capability makes it possible to capture these potential switchers without drawing too much attention.

A business can also focus on a margin of the market often called trendsetters, who are always looking for something new and interesting. A core capability or strength may be determined by the following questions:

    I.   Can the capability be easily imitated?

    II.   Is the capability durable or enduring?

    III.   Is it difficult to substitute?

IV.   Can it be applied to other markets?

V.   Does it give the business competitive superiority?

RECONFIGURING THE VALUE CHAIN

An entrepreneur can consider and observe the weakness in the process of delivering value to a customer. What are the specific areas within the value chain that can be changed or improved? By improving service delivery (faster, cheaper or better quality) an entrepreneur can gradually work towards building brand visibility specifically tied to whatever value they deliver to a customer. Reconfiguring the value chain may also mean asking the 9 Whats of problem solving:

I.   What can be substituted?

II.   What can be combined?

III.   What can be adapted?

IV.   What can I magnify?

V.   What can I modify?

VI.   What new ways can the idea be applied?

VII.   What can be eliminated?

VIII.   What can be rearranged?

47

IX.   What can be reversed?

LEVERAGING

As an entrepreneur discovers the potencies and strengths latent in their business, they can proceed to harness these assets and use them as the pivot to capture a portion of the market. The Phoenicians remained competent sea farers, whilst the Romans became skilled and innovative conquerors thereby advancing their agenda throughout the known world. It is imperative for entrepreneurs to discover and appreciate their strengths and most importantly their assets, and put them to effective use.

Armed with these simple but effective strategies entrepreneurs can emerge as the great modern day *strategoi*, renowned for great vision and strategic genius destined to conquer and establish great business empires.

CHOOSING YOUR STRATEGY TO SUIT YOUR TERRAIN

Strategy is a reflection of the general and the terrain he or she is navigating. In the article "Your Strategy Needs a Strategy", Martin Reeves, Claire Love, and Philipp Tillmanns state that there are two critical factors that determine strategy; malleability and predictability.[24] Predictability points to the general's ability to see into the future, and precision in forecasting or backcasting the outcomes and needs. Malleability points to how a competitor can influence the specific needs and outcomes of a particular industry. Reeves, Love and Tillmanns propose the following strategic styles:

I. **A classical strategy** works well for businesses that are operating in predictable and immutable environments. The normal practice in this case is to set a goal and then over time build and strengthen this position using certain internal capabilities. This strategy is for businesses operating in stable environments as change is slow, meaning there is sufficient time to make adjustments and changes to the strategy without losing too much ground.

II. **An adaptive strategy** is more flexible and experimental; it works far better in immutable environments that are unpredictable. This means

---

[24] Martin Reeves, *Your Strategy Needs A Strategy: How To Choose And Execute The Best Approach*, (Harvard Business Review Press)

an environment that is difficult to change but volatile. As an example Zimbabwe's economic environment, is presently immutable based on a number of factors both external and internal but it is highly volatile and unpredictable. In this case a business needs to be able to constantly refine goals and manoeuvre through fast changing conditions. The goal is to be me pliable.

III. **A shaping strategy** is best in unpredictable environments that you have the power to change. This strategy works well in environments that are prone to a lot of innovation and demand is difficult to predict. This means that planning and implementation cycles run for a shorter period of time.

IV. **A visionary strategy** (the build-it-and-they-will-come approach) is appropriate in predictable environments that you have the power to change. This is a very bold approach to strategy, pointing to the ability to not only predict the future but, to create it. The environment can be changed and the entrepreneur can change it.

To apply these strategies it is vital to know your industry and the broad conditions of its context. This helps to develop strategies that align the growth of your business to external conditions thereby creating the smoothest path towards victory.

THE HEART OF STRATEGY

Ultimately, the heart of a strategy is vested in the ability and skill to execute it. The character and personality of a general determines the outcome of war. It is a common occurrence in any industry for a good business idea to fail. This can be the result of factors such as the business model, timing and so forth. Nonetheless a victorious outcome can be narrowed down to the disposition, personality and decision making of the man or woman in charge.

5 TYPES OF STRATEGOI

THE ADVENTUROUS CONQUEROR: an individual who tolerates and pursues risk and always looks for new opportunities and challenges. They seek out growth and value speed in action and clarity of thought. They are flexible and adaptable to new technologies. Think Alexander the Great.

THE OPPORTUNIST: individuals who are fast followers and are and moderately risk-tolerant. By nature, they are imitators and focus on defence and attack. They ride and thrive on the adventurous conqueror's failures.

THE DEFENDER: an individual who is risk-averse and generally resistant to change. They are swift to respond to threats and potential attacks on their market share but, are not aggressive or proactive when it comes to new technologies. Very insular in nature meaning they focus on internal competencies.

THE SUBVERTER: this is an individual who thrives on the enemy's weakness from within and is prone to risk-taking. They are revolutionary and radical with disruptive tendencies. They react to situations and display a degree of cunning and shrewdness. They use diversionary and deflective approaches.

THE GUERRILLA: an individual who takes serious risks using diversionary and counterintuitive strategies. Avoids direct conflict and uses the element of surprise to great effect.

Thrives in situations and contexts with limited resources and uses unconventional approaches and methods to achieve results.

> Now the general is the bulwark of the State (business); if the bulwark is complete at all points; the State will be strong; if the bulwark is defective, the State will be weak.[25]
>
> Sun Tzu

At the heart of a strong state is a strong general. As it is with the State, so it is with any business. The general or *strategoi* is the leader who steers the ship. If the entrepreneur is weak and indecisive it will naturally follow that the business will be weak and defective. Hence it is imperative that strategy be the centrepiece of any enterprise for the following:

I.   **Dealing with problems and risks:** Strategy helps an entrepreneur analyse customer needs and issues prevailing within a particular industry as well as design the innovative solutions to deliver value.

---

25 Sun Tsu, *The Art of War*,3

II.   **Pursuing a particular agenda or direction:** Strategy is useful in the surge forward to an end goal or vision.

III.   **Initiating offensive action in the market:** It is the core activity that leads to success or failure in accessing the market and achieving growth.

> War, or any kind of conflict, is waged and won through strategy. Think of strategy as a series of lines and arrows aimed at a goal: at getting you to a certain point in the world, at helping you to attack a problem in your path, at figuring out how to encircle and destroy your enemy. Before directing these arrows at your enemies, however, you must first direct them at yourself.[26]
>
> Robert Greene

The decisive moments in any war, come down to the confidence and resolve of the general in battle. The morale of the army and the willingness to surge forward are driven by the faith of the soldiers in the decision making and courage of their general. Therefore the most

---

[26] Robert Greene, *The 33 Strategies of War*, (Profile Books 2010), 1

important battle that an entrepreneur must face is the battle within.

Before taking on the market and the world the entrepreneur must face the enemy within. Some of the greatest encumbrances faced by entrepreneurs are internal. Everything from anxiety, fear, and worry affect the quality of strategic thought. Hence to effectively engage in clear and poignant strategic thought, war must be waged against negative thinking.

8 THOUGHTS OF A VICTORIOUS GENERAL'S MIND-SET

i. **Think of Success:** Success is a pattern of thinking it begins in the mind.

ii. **Increase your expectations:** generate ideas that stretch you and expand your horizons

iii. **Positive results from positive actions**: Set your mind to perform to the best of your abilities

iv. **Choose to be in control:** how you respond to chaos, disappointment, and failure is a choice.

v. **Be responsible for your actions:** no one can bear the burden of the steps you took to walk out of the door.

vi.   **Make no excuses for lack of results**: nothing can stop you from getting a result except thoughts of failure before an action.

vii.   **Be Proactive in the face of change:** Change is inevitable, so too the results of indecision and inaction in the midst of or prior to change.

viii. **Be Victor of circumstance**: see your environment and challenges as the podium for your victory.

THE THREE A'S OF THE MASTER STRATEGIST

The object of a great general is not the glory and grandiose plaudits of his peers and enemies but to achieve the intended goal.

Historians postulate that Leonidas held the position at the Hot Gates for strategic purposes and not for glory because he was a pragmatic and well-rounded Spartan general who engendered the values and traditions of the Spartan way of life. Robert Greene proposes the following steps to become a strategist of renown.[27]

---

[27] Robert Greene, *The 33 Strategies of War*

I. **Awareness**: Introspection, analysis, and wise counsel uncover the weakness and ailments that arrest the mind, dulling strategic powers. Sun Tzu and Aristotle advocate that we must know ourselves. Strong self-awareness helps to build the necessary courage to take on challenges. The hardest thing we will ever do is not to lead an army into battle and victory or run a business into profit. The hardest thing that we will ever do is to lead ourselves. Self-leadership is an all-day everyday task throughout life.

II. **Attack**: Declare war on the things inside you that hinder you from moving move forward. Face your worst fears especially of the future, to surge ahead with a particular course of action. I love Aragorn's brave proclamation in **The Lord of the Rings**, "I do not fear death" as he enters through the door made by the dead.[28] To move forward we must first move within. The longest journey is between the heart and the mind. Once we overcome the

---

[28] John Ronald Reuel Tolkien, The Lord of the Rings: Volume One

conflict between desire and reason we can take on the world.

III.   **Attrition**: Wage ruthless and continual battle on the enemies within you, by applying certain strategies. Attrition, in this case, means slowly chipping away at weaknesses by choosing to grow and move forward and resisting the temptation to give up or surrender. Continuous improvement is a concept that has shaped the world's cultures over millennia and it has influenced business over the centuries in the form of the Japanese concept of Kaizen. Essentially, it must shape individual growth.

A prince or general who knows exactly how to organise his war according to his object and means, who does neither too little nor too much, gives by that the greatest proof of his genius. But the effects of this talent are exhibited not so much by the invention of new modes of action, which might strike the eye immediately, as in the successful final result of the whole. It is the exact fulfilment of silent suppositions, it is the noiseless harmony of the whole action which we should admire, and which only makes itself known in the total result. [29]

Claus von Clausewitz

The wonder of a strategy is not seen in the development of great innovations, creative and tactical actions but in the overall outcome of all intents and actions which, is profit. The great generals are best remembered for the outcomes and significance of their actions. I often say, "Don't over celebrate winning a battle before the war is won."

And this is best encapsulated by Claus von Clausewitz when he says, "It is the exact fulfilment of silent suppositions, it is the noiseless harmony of the whole action which we should admire, and which only makes itself known in the total result."

The greatest impression we should draw from the Roman *Corvus* is that they finally defeated the Phoenicians and the *onager* contributed to the overall pursuit of Pax Romana.

---

[29] Carl von Clausewitz, *On War - Completed: Great Essays*, (2016)

Though the *Corvus* and *onager* were impressive innovations their significance could only be measured by their contribution to the intended outcome shaped by the decisions and concerted actions of great generals.

Chapter 5 THE NEED FOR A VISION

AND A GOAL

There's a famous proverb in the Bible that says, "Where there is no vision the people cast off restraint."[30] This proverb implies that, where no vision exists there is no self-control, no underlying focus to help people navigate through life.

It is, therefore, quite a serious thing for an individual or business to have no vision. Helen Keller born blind was asked, "What could be worse than being born blind?" She replied, "To have sight without vision."[31]

The loss of self-control and focus inevitably results in a state of chaos and disorder. Interestingly, the *Catapult Effect* puts strategy before vision against the normal practice because as discussed earlier, strategy is about the individual or the person and the way they think.

---

[30] Proverbs 29:18 New International Version (NIV)
[31] Dale E. Galloway *Confidence Without Conceit*, (F.H. Revell,1989),55

It is from this basis that vision can emerge when an entrepreneur has the capacity to think through and shape the vision and goal for their business. Before one has a vision it is imperative that they be capable of thinking differently.

Vision emerges out of a deep and perceptive thought process. In Ancient Greece, it was imperative to have a man who was capable of leading the men into battle, before the objectives and intents of war were discussed. It is pointless to develop a vision that will be poorly executed.

Entrepreneurs need a vision and a goal. They need to see the desired outcome and the means to get there one step at a time. Vision and goals create the springboard from which they can launch into the market with the necessary focus and self-control to achieve Sustainable Competitive Advantage.

Vision will be derived from an appreciation of certain aspects of the current state and the desired future. A third of planning and visioning must be dedicated to appreciating the past and present and two-thirds dedicated to shaping the future. The future of your business can be one of six different perspectives set out by Dr. Sohail Inayatullah and reconsidered in this chapter.[32]

I. **Used future**: Is the future of your business borrowed from another? Are you following the pattern set out by another firm that has already blazed the path you are intending to walk? The conflict around patents between Samsung and Apple came down to a claim of originality. The who-copied-who question was answered by the courts but the bottom-line speaks volumes as to who borrowed a used future.

II. **Disowned future**: Is your future dependent on your skills, neglecting all other possibilities? Is there room for learning and developing other competencies? This is one of the aspects at the core of Clayton Christensen's book the *Innovator's Dilemma* when good businesses fail.[33]

[32] Sohail Inayatullah, *Six pillars: Futures Thinking For Transforming*, accessed 12 December 2018. www.benlandau.com
[33] Clayton M. Christensen, *The Innovators Dilemma : When New Technologies Cause Great Firms To Fail* (Harvard Business Review Press 2015)

III. **Alternative future**: Is your future a blank canvas upon which you want to paint what you have imagined? Though it is likely that there's one destination, are there different means by which to get there?

IV. **Models of Social change:** Is your future inevitable (e.g. doomed to fail) or is it a proactive outcome of a desire to participate in the transformation of your environment?

V. **Alignment:** Is your future inextricably tied to your plan (strategy) for the future? Do your day to day activities tie into your plan for the future and how you intend to get there? Is there something 'larger than life' about you and your business?

VI. **Uses of the future:** Having given it careful consideration, can you confidently shape your future and the future of your environment?

Your vision is influenced by what are called drivers. There are four generic drivers of the future. Drivers can be defined as particular things or occurrences that have a significant effect on the outcome of the future.

I. **Events**: Things that happened in the past, things happening at present and things that are going to happen in the future.

II. **Trends**: The continual occurrence of particular events in a general way as to form a definite direction and pattern.

III. **Discontinuities**: Volatile and unpredictable disruptions in the way things are done by someone or something.

IV. **Milestone**: A significant mark or point highlighting a new development or stage in a business or individual's life. Milestones are indicators of breakthroughs and results of revolutionary and innovative actions over time.

WHAT IS YOUR VISION AND GOAL FOR THE FUTURE?

The answer can be broad and spread across different aspects of life or can be more specific to an area like business. The vision and goals of an entrepreneur give us a glimpse into the possible future of the business and therefore require much consideration and thought in developing them.

SIX KEYS FOR ESTABLISHING A VISION

I. What is your intended desire for the future?

II. What are the facts relating to what you see? Find all the available data and information relating to your vision.

III. Identify the problems and potential threats and challenges you may face.

IV. Consider and explore as many solutions for the problems you discover.

V. Examine and re-examine all possible solutions to find a workable option.

VI. This ensures that you have a vision and the desired result (goal).

THE IMPACT OF VISION

A story is told by Josephus the Jewish historian that Alexander the Great, having conquered the great empire of Persia in 333 B.C. at age 20, sought to attack Egypt. [34] As he travelled through Syria on his way to Egypt he decided to besiege Jerusalem. Upon hearing that

---

[34] Alonzo T. Jones, *The Great Empires of Prophecy: From Babylon To The Fall Of Rome*, (Teach Services Incorporated 2014)

Alexander was approaching Jerusalem, a wise old priest called Jaddua approached him carrying Daniel's prophecies from the Bible.

As the story goes, Alexander explained to the priest a dream he had earlier of meeting an old man dressed in white who was going to tell him something very significant. Jaddua went on to read Daniel's visions of the future.

Alexander saw clearly that he was the powerful he-goat represented in the prophecy that would destroy the Medo-Persian Empire and conquer the world. This vision changed the course of history as Alexander the Great went on to conquer the entire known world before his death at age 33.

> The great tomorrows are bestowed to those that see them.
>
> Anonymous

This story reveals the value of the right vision in shaping an entrepreneur's business and potentially shaping the history of a society. It also reveals the importance of thinking and dreaming big. To achieve greatness one must be able to see it.

SMARTEST GOAL SETTING

Once you've developed a vision with a clear picture of tomorrow it is important to develop goals to achieve it. Consider what small steps you need to take to establish your business and make it a household name. What are the most important things that need to be done to ensure success?

It is generally proposed and accepted that goals ought to be SMART; **S**pecific, **M**easurable, **A**ttainable, **R**ealistic and **T**ime-bound.

I believe it is possible to develop SMARTEST goals that are **S**pecific, **M**easurable, **A**ttainable, **R**ealistic, **T**ime-bound, **E**xcellent, **S**ignificant and **T**imeless.

By adding three more important aspects to your goal setting framework. The extra elements ensure that an entrepreneur focuses on aspects that ultimately translate to significance.

- **Excellent**: Goals should be set at exceptional standards in terms of quality and overall ingenuity. The brilliance of ancient generals was solely a credit of their ingenuity and intent. Consider Hannibal of Carthage's goal to attack Rome. Not only was his goal SMART, it was also excellent. It showed ambition as well as ingenuity affording Hannibal renown as a great military strategist. The brilliance of his strategy was that Rome was not expecting the attack and was never in a position to counter it.

- **Significant**: Business as with war is designed to achieve a level of significance. Few people in this world pursue ignominy and insignificance. We all want to be remembered for something or by someone. We want our lives to have meaning. SMARTEST goals drive a business to consider the extent to which a goal contributes to the overall success and significance of the business.

- **Timeless**: Although a goal has a specific time frame within which it must be completed it also has a degree of impact. There are goals and actions that will reverberate through time and history. We can choose to set goals that not only scare us but challenge us to build and design products and businesses that contribute to a larger than life vision.

SMARTEST goal setting branches further beyond creating efficient, effective and achievable goals. It initiates the process of building legacies. It is the point at which an individual or organisation begin to create and implement goals that influence the legacy they leave behind.

I believe the most profound and satisfying experience is to achieve goals that are timeless in their impact. It is imperative therefore that an individual or organisation visualise a significant end.

Consider the shout of Maximus in Ridley Scott's Gladiator, "What we do in this life echoes into eternity."[35] SMARTEST goals are the founding blocks and milestones that shape a life full of purpose and meaning.

As Maya Angelou once said, "Life is not measured by the number of breaths we take but by the number of moments that take our breath away."[36] In business,

---

[35]   http://afrikanknight.blogspot.com/2012/10/imaginationis-more-important-than
[36] Melanie Young, *Follow Your Dreams*,(Lulu.com 2013)

SMARTEST goal setting yields continuous profits, lasting employee and customer experiences that will ultimately impact the nation.

THREE MODELS OF THINKING

Whatever challenges we face and no matter the size of the competitor, it is possible to overcome them with the right vision and goals. Ari Wallach in his article *How to Think like a Futurist* proposes three transformative ways to think that can help develop future focused visions and goals.[37]

I.   **Trans-generational thinking:** Like Pericles we need to think of future generations when we develop business ideas. Wars at times were fought for posterity to save and defend the heirloom. Great kings and generals went to war because they could see the possibility of their kingdoms being conquered by savage oppressors in the future. The great businesses of our time like Disney were built

---

[37] Ari Wallach, *How To Think Like A Futurist* Date accessed: 11 December 2018. https://ideas.ted.com/three-ways-to-think-about-the-future

by trans-generational thinkers who built for their children and their children's future.

II. **Futures thinking:** The idea of multiple futures or alternative futures helps us to see that most problems and challenges aren't simplistic. Thus before going to war for a hill it is important to determine possible scenarios and outcomes of that singular action. Futures thinking challenges the entrepreneur to see and unlock different scenarios and alternative futures at play.

III. *Telos:* Is a Greek word that refers to the ultimate purpose or aim of something.[38] Before pursuing a business idea it is essential to consider the ultimate aim. Some wars were pursued for aimless ends and this was often only discovered after many lives had been lost. As Simon Sinek states, "People always buy why you do what you do."[39] *Telos* challenges the entrepreneur to design businesses with a clear and definitive end game in mind.

---

[38] https://en.wikipedia.org/wiki/Telos Date accessed 20 December 2018
[39] Simon Sinek, *Start With Why* (Portfolio/Penguin 2011)

CHASE WHAT YOU SEE

Ultimately, in our endeavours to become successful entrepreneurs, we must have,

I. **A DEEP SEATED DESIRE TO EXCEL:** If you have low expectations and ambitions for life, it is easy to settle for something lower than your potential. A good vision is shaped and crafted by what you expect to give the world and what you are expecting in return.

II. **A TRAJECTORY THAT GOES BEYOND SUCCESS TOWARDS SIGNIFICANCE:** We all want our lives to have meaning. It's not enough to simply attain a measure of success. All champions want to win more than once for the express reason that they aspire to be significant. Our lives must count for something more than a statistic in a textbook.

III. **THE BURNING PASSION FACTOR:** good vision is shaped by an unflinching and dogged passion for whatever problem or challenge you are trying to solve. As the common adage goes Rome was not built in a day, rather good vision is tapered by your dedication and desire to see it fulfilled in your lifetime and beyond.

IV.   **A LONG TERM AND ETERNAL PERSPECTIVE:** "What we do on this earth echoes into eternity." The words of Maximus in the movie the Gladiator. A long term and eternal perspective engenders a sense of purpose beyond ourselves. When we shape vision it must at least be trans-generational. Our thoughts must be for our great grandchildren. It is not enough to have a vision that perishes when we perish with the eulogium, "Here lies an entrepreneur who had a dream to change the world but died with it!"

DARE TO SEE BEYOND YOURSELF!

THE PATH TO SIGNIFICANCE

The path to significance is arduous and requires an entrepreneur to persevere through different situations. The great empires of old were built on the foundation of successes and failures with an ardent pursuit of destiny. These four ingredients determine the kind of vision and goals we develop and whether we uncover the glorious trajectory towards significance.

I. **THE VALLEY**: Always start from the bottom. Empires have been born out of hardship and difficulty. See the world empathetically embracing challenges, problems and goodness with equal weighting. Viktor Frankl says, "Can life retain its potential meaning in spite of its tragic aspects?"[40] The valley points to the inception and early stage level of your business, when nothing is easy.

II. **THE CLIFF OF SUCCESS**: Inevitably ardent and passionate pursuit of a clear vision with practical goals leads to success. Yet success for the sake of it is never the destination. The greatest danger for an entrepreneur is to camp in the exhilaration of one victory whilst still at war. Success can easily be the plateau for most businesses as they lavish in positive cash flows without paying attention to the shifting needs of the market.

---

[40] Victor E. Frankl, *Man's Search For Meaning*, (Beacon Press 2006)

III.   **THE PEAK OF SIGNIFICANCE**: The substance of a great vision and strong goals is expressly for the purpose of achieving value and worth. No venture should descend into the pits of meaningless and vainglorious pursuits; for to do so may also be considered a waste. The journey of great generals should reverberate with the journey of a great entrepreneur in that great victories ultimately serve a greater purpose. We must build businesses that last.

IV.   **SKY IS THE LIMIT:** Entrepreneurs must ride the wave of significance. The three models of thinking help an entrepreneur harness and design opportunities that transcend generations, spread across geographies, enrich and embed in the memories of people and almost cheat time. The world makes way for the entrepreneur who dares to build a legacy by pursuing the things that matter and make a difference.

DON'T PLAY SMALL

Without vision and clear goals, entrepreneurs run the risk of developing businesses that in the words of Robert D. Abrahams in his poem *The Night They Burned Shanghai* "...perish inch by inch playing little games". My passion and the object of this book is that entrepreneurs attain to significance.

"Some men die by shrapnel,

Some men go down in flames

But most men perish inch by inch, by playing little games."[41]

Robert D. Abrahams

[41] Robert D Abrahams *How They Burned Shangai* Date accessed: 12 December 2018.
http://www.bridgeguys.com/sec/poems/collection/TheNightTheyBurnedShanghai

Chapter 6   MAINTAINING THE GOAL(S)

Every successful military campaign was the result of small strategic and visionary steps in the right direction. Many of the greatest generals (*strategoi*) who did not shrink back in the face of adversity or defeat, chose to continue pursuing what they believed was their destiny by maintaining the goals they had set.

> An idea not coupled with action will never get any
> bigger than the brain cell it occupied.[42]

Arnold Glasow

You may have a solid base to launch from, great strategic thought, nonetheless if there is no determined action to move forward and attain to the greatness a vision and related goals to achieve it and all planning proves ineffective. One of the most profound goals in military history was Hannibal's attempts to attack Rome by

---

[42] Sharkie Zartman, *Shark Sense: Getting In Touch With Your Inner Shark,* (iUniverse 2011)

crossing the Alps. Hannibal had a clear vision and a clear goal, yet he faced significant obstacles in his pursuit of both. He had 6 main challenges

I.   *The Alps Mountains*: The mountain range was a formidable obstacle which eventually encouraged Hannibal to leave behind his siege engines and elephants.

II. *He would likely be outnumbered*: His goal to attack Rome meant he would inevitably have less troops because the Romans had home advantage.

III. *To get to Rome he had to go through Roman territory*: He had to march through enemy territory to get to Rome.

IV. *The encumbrance of too many resources*:   To achieve the level of speed and efficiency Hannibal had to outflank the Romans, Hannibal had to leave his siege-works and some of his elephants.

V.   *Hostile tribes*: As Hannibal marched through enemy territory he was likely going to face hostility from the citizens of Italy.

VI. *Weather*: Whether during his ascent of the Alps or his engagements with the enemy in Italy, weather was going to affect his advances.

There are a few reflections in this chapter that are important factors in ensuring that once the rubber hits the road the wheels keep turning and never fall off. A friend of mine Tendai Tsodzai used to like saying that, "A rolling stone gathers no moss?"

THE SIX ELEMENTS OF SUSTAINING GROWTH AND ADVANCEMENT

DETERMINATION

This is one of the most important attributes necessary to ensure that an entrepreneur maintains the right course towards a desired end or fulfilled vision. Any vision can be achieved by small or large concerted steps towards the prescribed destination. These are often called goals.

It's imperative that we learn to maintain clarity of purpose, remembering why you're in business to begin with and what you have been aiming for. Determination is also about perseverance, doggedly grabbing hold of tomorrow, today. Over the years I have appreciated and valued determination and perseverance as key ingredients for success in any endeavour.

Hannibal's attack of Rome was not hindered by the fact that he had a large physical barrier before him. When faced with the Alps his determination was signified by his choice to ascend the mountain. There was a clear and positive emotional feeling and action that drove him towards achieving a difficult goal in spite of a seemingly insurmountable obstacle. Maintaining the goal is about how much you want to achieve something and the level of determination is revealed when you face a significant obstacle or challenge.

Focus

There is a common feature among entrepreneurs to which I have often fallen prey. In military terms it is common to speak of diversionary tactics or the application of a decoy. In business it may be understood as strategic drift. Simply put it is a distraction – a castle in the clouds as it were. It is that moment when someone loses sight of the intended goal, and ends up pursuing something altogether irrelevant and unnecessary. It may be a lucrative deal or a 'quick buck' scheme, but it is common to hear of and see entrepreneurs pursue an 'illusory dream' outside their visionary path.

It is important that an entrepreneur learn to recognise "castles in the clouds" or diversionary tactics from an enemy (competitor) or self-perpetuated through desperation. Focus ensures that you don't waste valuable time and resources on things that never fulfil your vision or build your business. Furthermore, it ensures you remain on the straight and narrow path towards greatness.

During his many battles with the Romans on his way to Rome Hannibal encountered a general called Fabius Verrucosus who was eventually called "the delayer" because of the tactics he applied. [43] Instead of engaging in face to face combat Fabius would strategically place his armies in positions that hindered Hannibal from attacking or retreating. His goal was to wear Hannibal

---

[43] Bernard Mineo, *A Companion To Livy*, (John Wiley & Sons 2014) 182

down. What kept Hannibal going? He was a man with clear intentions and single minded devotion.

SEIZE AND MANAGE OPPORTUNITY

Carpe diem, as quoted from Horace is a common phrase in modern management and motivation language meaning, "seize the day or the moment." [44]May I put it to you that not every opportunity is for seizing. In fact, there are opportunities we must learn to pass up. That's why it's important to manage opportunity. I often ask the following questions to test if an opportunity is in line with my vision.

I.   Is the opportunity compatible to my goals and objectives?

II. Is the opportunity in line with my values and ethics?

III. Do I have the necessary skills to execute it?

IV. Do I have the capacity and resources to meet the expectations?

V.   Do I have the inspiration and passion to see the opportunity to its end?

---

[44] Horace, Horace Odes I: Carpe Diem (Clarendon Press 1995)

VI.   If the answer is no to 3, 4 and 5 can I obtain the capacity or can I develop the necessary inspiration and competence?

When Hannibal was within striking distance of Rome, he had a great opportunity to attack Rome. But the reality was that he didn't have sufficient resources to launch the attack and his army was exhausted from the previous battle.

Sometimes when a great opportunity presents itself the issue comes down to having the necessary ingredients to launch a successful attack on a competitor. As difficult as it sounds sometimes the perfect opportunity may come at the wrong time. Like Hannibal it may mean holding off and delaying gratification.

The concept of *carpe futura* which means seize the future implies that every opportunity laid before you, must align to your desired future and end. The Roman Empire is a great example of the contribution of small battles to the ultimate vision of *Pax Romana*. It was the minute details of Caesar's strategy to spread the idea of Rome that drove their advancement into different territories and ultimately establishing an empire that lasted 1500 years.[45]

HANDLE DISAPPOINTMENT

The hardest thing I have encountered in my life as an entrepreneur is facing and dealing with disappointment. It irritates the best of us and haunts and plagues the weakest among us. Yet, the reality is that it is a very prominent and extant part of the human experience. We inevitably face disappointment at some point in life and in business, through our own failures or the failures of others.

In maintaining a goal, the ability and skill to move forward in the face of disappointment is imperative if not critical. And by moving forward, I mean doing so with no regrets or grudges, as these simply drag you back to the past each time something goes wrong.

Defeat is a reality of war but it can be minimized by how we handle it. The most successful generals in theory and practice accepted the reality of failure and uncovered ways to mitigate it. Having an air of invincibility or a 'know-

---

[45] D.H. Green, *Language and History In The Early Germanic World* (Cambridge University Press 2000) 44

it-all' attitude can be deceptive. Rather, what is more powerful is the ability to face the reality of failure and defeat with humility and fortitude. In this way you are positioned better for victory.

Four Powers of Equanimity

When a person has the capacity to handle success, failure with equal temperance they have the quality of equanimity. This means they can weigh information with an even mind and uncover the reality. There are Four powers of equanimity that will help an entrepreneur navigate their way out of disappointment and failure.

I.   Power of Objectivity in crisis
II. Power of Awareness in any given situation
III. Power of Acceptance in different circumstances
IV. Power of Decisiveness in defeat or victory

What makes Hannibal a great general, was that when he was finally defeated and the Second Punic war ended in 201BC, he humbly took on the post of Chief Magistrate. [46]He performed his duties with the same standard of

---

[46] John Francis Lazenby, Hannibals War: Mllitray History of the Second Punic War (University of Oklahoma Press, 1998)

excellence he had applied as a military commander so much that the heavy taxes that were imposed by Rome to curtail Carthaginian ambitions were paid with ease. For an entrepreneur, if defeat and failure means finding a new opportunity or getting a job, the spirit and energy of entrepreneurship must not diminish rather it must flourish.

FACE YOUR FEARS AND ANXIETIES

Aragorn in the movie Lord of the Rings, walks through the gate made by the dead with the bold whisper, "I do not fear death." [47]For many of us, it is important to face our fears, as these are often obstacles and hindrances that block our paths towards success. In creative thinking there's a technique called boundary relaxation.

It is designed to test the boundaries we build around us, real and imagined. Fears and anxieties are generally imagined boundaries that don't exist. Jesus taught a simple truth when he said, "Don't worry about tomorrow." [48] What He is saying is don't concern yourself too much

[47] John Ronald Reuel Tolkien, The Lord Of The Rings: Volume One (Houghton Mifflin Harcourt,2012)
[48] Matthew 6:34 New International Version (NIV)

with things you cannot control. Instead, manage tomorrow by acting today.

Inaction is often caused by anxiety and fear. Often when an entrepreneur is unable to make a decision it is very likely that they are afraid of, or anxious about the potential outcome. Hence, action and the ability to maintain a goal arise from facing fear and anxiety.

I believe the downfall of most generals is as a result of fear. It is one of chief causes of dulling one's strategic faculties. The simple reason is that fear disables and leads to indecision and double mindedness. Thus in the midst of battle, fear is what results in miscalculations and unnecessary tactical manoeuvres.

COMBAT ENDURANCE

According to Wikipedia citing Leonard, Barry (2011) Combat endurance is the time that a military system or unit can remain in combat before having to withdraw due to depleted resources.[49]Through obvious and simple

---

[49] Leonard Barry. Date accessed 12 December 2018. https://en.wikipedia.org/wiki/Combat_endurance

observations it is clear that after about one hour of intense physical exertion, performance is likely to diminish.

This is the same case with battles during times of war. Ancient warriors had many things to contend with besides surviving the battle, like access to sufficient food, heavy equipment and travelling long distances. How long can your business survive whilst attacking the market? This is a time that must be determined.

The 4 Modicums of Combat Endurance in Business

Combat endurance within the business landscape can be determined by the following modicums:

I. Sufficient cash flows to sustain business development and marketing campaigns. One of the biggest challenges in war and in business is access to money. An entrepreneur must determine the amount of cash required through planning to sustain an attack on a market. One of the pitfalls of Hannibal's campaign was that when he finally got close to Rome he didn't have the 'cash flow' to initiate the final attack.

II.   Sufficient and multi-skilled human resources that can adapt to shifting conditions in the market. One of the things Hannibal did to build more resources was to attract fighting talent from the cities of Italy who were looking to be liberated from Rome.

III. Sufficient product or productive capacity to meet demand in the event the customer base increases significantly.

IV.   Sufficient tactical prowess to counter retaliatory attacks from a competitor. Hannibal had sufficient strategic and tactical skill to counter the onslaughts of his Roman enemy. The success of any enterprise will be determined by the strength of the general (*strategoi*) and their ability to manoeuvre in hostile conditions.

ROME WAS NOT BUILT IN A DAY

An entrepreneur must always remember that, 'Rome was not built in a day,' rather, it was built over centuries by generals and emperors with one vision and goal in mind, '*Pax Romana*' Roman peace throughout the known world.

Whether in a century or in six months, the success of your business is established by dogged determination, focus, seizing and managing opportunity, handling disappointment, facing fears and anxieties and most importantly combat endurance.

> "Pursue your goal relentlessly because consistency is the only currency for success."
>
> Anonymous

Chapter 7 INITIATING OFFENSIVE ACTION – THE MVP

> The overthrow of the enemy is the aim in war; destruction of the hostile military forces, the means both in attack and defence. By the destruction of the enemy's military force, the defensive is led on to the offensive, the offensive is led by it to the conquest of territory.[50]
>
> Claus von Clausewitz

The express objects of war and business are similar - victory and profit. To achieve profit within a market is to be in possession of market share. Yet, the one thing every entrepreneur must accept when they start a business is that they are recognized as an entrant into a specific market or as a challenger.

This means that they are in a vulnerable position from the onset. Statistically, new businesses and entrepreneurs have a high failure rate and it's often agreed that most

---

[50] Carl von Clausewitz, *On War - Completed: Great Essays.*

new businesses won't survive the first three to five years. If this is the case then entrepreneurs need to develop strategies for survival and more importantly for growth.

The 5th principle of The *Catapult Effect* considers the importance of offensive action. Every entrepreneur must have a plan and offensive route to market. There are 3 aspects necessary when an entrepreneur considers offensive action. It is important to note that offensive action means laying siege to an incumbent's market share which could result in a counter attack. So what must an entrepreneur consider?

LAUNCHING YOUR PRODUCT AND IDEAS INTO THE MARKET FAST

> Unless important advantages are to be gained from hesitation, it is necessary to set to work at once.[51]
>
> Claus von Clausewitz

---

[51] Ibid

Why hesitate or delay? Unless there is a clear benefit in delaying the product launch, it is highly imperative that an entrepreneur go on the offensive. It is for the sake of the business that offensive action must be initiated. It is never enough to have an impressive product sitting on the shelf. Rather, the true value of a product is measured by the value generated by customer actions.

And the only way to find out if the customer is interested is to go to market. The hallmark of great victories was the concerted and intentional march of an army on the battlefield, instead of staying cooped up in the barracks or being engaged in civilian affairs in the city. Whether the aim is to grab 2% of the market, 80% or attain a monopoly the point of initiating offensive action is the same.

A popular mantra in business is 'first mover advantage' meaning whoever has the product or service that satisfies a customer's pressing needs, grabs the market. To achieve first mover advantage, entrepreneurs must create and launch a product at the lowest cost and in the shortest time possible way (according to industry standards) whilst under the radar.

A minimum viable product would be a solution to a problem that may not be perfect but meets some of the customer's key needs. Furthermore, an entrepreneur needs to establish the customer base the big player in the industry isn't really interested in. Finding this small niche of the market share provides the entrepreneur the opportunity to test their product and receive the necessary feedback and uplift without courting too much attention.

FOUR KEYS OF STRATEGIC TARGETING

Your vision might be taking Mount Everest but your steps must take into account overcoming the perils of other surrounding peaks and valleys or at least having the aerial power to challenge for the high places in the market. Beyond market share an entrepreneur should aim for market space. There are four keys to consider:

I. **Profitability**: Profitability is a matter of combining quality, price and customer perception with the necessary experience to develop the right product to market fit over time. The formula for profitability takes into consideration the revenues generated from pushing your product, the cost of developing and marketing your product, the margins that can be attained and lastly resource velocity that is the rate at which you can produce products based on an amount invested within a certain time frame.

II. **Competitiveness**: Importantly the aim of designing a good product is to provide the customer with unique value more superior to the competitor's.

III. **Customer Centric**: Great businesses are established by understanding customer needs through immersing all business activities in deliberate and focused interactions with the customer. It is not merely the power of new technologies or unique business models that results in success. Of principal importance is an appreciation of customer need independent of the solution you offer.

IV. **Cost Effectiveness:** Achieving optimal levels of performance in pursuit of the most beneficial value propositions for your customer. How can you improve the organisation? How can you access and use better knowledge? How can you improve actions within the business? How can you improve ongoing effort and sustainability (continuous improvement)?

CREATING THE NECESSARY STRATEGIES TO SUPPORT THE GROWTH OF YOUR BUSINESS

An important aspect to secure success in an enterprise is an eye on the pulse of the market and discerning the times and winds of change. As times and seasons shift small businesses have one advantage over bigger organisations with more complex decision making hierarchies - flexibility. It points to the ability to shift and act on an opportunity when it arises without the encumbrances of bureaucracy.

Yet, flexibility is only an advantage if an entrepreneur has an eye on the market and the ability to recognize when times change. Any change presents opportunities and threats and entrepreneurs must be positioned to recognize these changes and seize any opportunities to emerge. It's important to have a plan of action and it's also critical to keep planning i.e. assessing your current state in light of your intended future state. The decline of the Phoenicians can be attributed to their inability to adapt to the Roman application of the *corvus* at sea.

FOUR DIAGNOSTIC QUESTIONS FOR ATTACKING THE MARKET

> The overthrow of the enemy is the aim in war; destruction of the hostile military forces, the means both in attack and defence.[52]
>
> Claus von Clausewitz

To achieve profitability and success, an entrepreneur must prize market share from a competitor or substitute. A great general's conquest is to use attack as a means to win over territory. Yet, naturally territory is always occupied by someone else. The four diagnostic questions below help an entrepreneur determine the value and quality of the opportunity.

---

[52] Carl von Clausewitz, *On War - Completed: Great Essays*

I. Is the idea competitive and relevant to your market? This explores the degree to which a product meets the customer's need.

II. Does your product clearly solve a problem or does it explore new ways of doing things? This tests the innovativeness of the product both as a solution and approach to customer behaviour.

III. Is your product or service feasible, saleable and viable? This explores the practicality, appeal and potential success of a product in the market.

IV. Do you have a plan of action to launch and maintain your product in the market place? Ensuring there is clear strategic thought and action that will translate to profitability.

TYPES OF OFFENSIVE STRATEGIES

Dr. Peter Yannopoulos proposes the following attack strategies:

I. **Launch a frontal attack**: Take your competitor head on especially if you have the capacity and the confidence that victory is certain. This isn't often recommended for entrants but may work if the entrepreneur has a game changer. Naturally the frontal attack of a competitor requires the necessary resource to defeat them. The wisdom of Jesus adequately captures the need to assess your capacity to attack a stronger competitor.

Or what king, going to encounter another king in war, will not sit down first and take counsel whether he is able with ten thousand men to meet him who comes against him with twenty thousand.[53]

Jesus

II. **Launch a flanking attack**: Finding the path of least resistance and exploiting the competitor's weakness. In many cases this is one of the best routes for entering a market, drawing attention but outflanking the incumbent.

III. **Launch a guerrilla attack**: Used by much smaller companies to keep the incumbent guessing when or where the next attack will happen. An entrepreneur engaging a guerrilla attack

---

[53] Luke 14:31 King James Version (KJV)

leverages their size to be viewed as inconsequential and invisible as they move amongst the customers.

a. **FIND THE EXCITING:** Find the aspects of your business, product or brand that excite your customers.

b. **BE CREATIVE:** Generate marketing and business development ideas that have a WOW effect to get your audience's attention.

c. **CONTENT IS KING:** Create online and offline content that inspires them to share it with someone else.

d. **CATAPULT:** Leverage these networks to increase the number of people who see your content and to widen your reach.

e. **EFFICIENCY:** USE these network effects to lower the people to cost rate for your campaigns.

f. **INNOVATION:** Focus on and use low cost marketing tools to generate maximum effect.

The guerrilla must move amongst the people as a fish swims in the sea.[54]

Mao Zedong.

IV. **Engage in strategic encirclement:** It is often a very expensive and expansive initiative if you are to surround the competitor. This is an ambitious strategy and requires the levels of investment and resources that give an entrepreneur economies of scale.

V. **Seeking undefended markets:** Bypass the competitor totally and seek untested markets and gain first mover advantage. This is one of the best strategies for entrepreneurs and points to the entrepreneur's ability to innovate as well as recognise undesired but valuable opportunity.

   a. Develop Clear market parameters
   b. Assess Key attributes and statistics of the market.
   c. Competitive analysis of market incumbents and Key demographics

---

[54] Mao Tse-tung *On Guerilla Warfare*, (Courier Corporation 2012)

d. Growth potential of market

e. Defensive positions in the market

f. Innovation potential

g. Ecosystem (parallel technologies) to support industry or market development

VI. **The predatory strategy:** Accepting lower profits to deter competitors. This requires that an entrepreneur have the capacity and resources to sustain low margins.

VII. **The underdog strategy:** This is especially effective when a small company enters a market where the incumbent is bureaucratic and unresponsive to client needs. It takes a bit more courage but can lead to exciting results. In essence the incumbent and market as a whole underestimates the true potential of the entrepreneur.

VIII. **The Judo strategy:** This strategy entails using the incumbent's weight against them in the same way as it is done in the martial art. The most fascinating thing about Judo is the paradoxical nature of attack. It is in the same mould as a ploy. When one seems to be in defence it is often the most opportune time to attack. This is because the full thrust of your enemy can be used against them. There are three ways to use Judo in a business context:

    a. **Attack weakness with strength**: Find your competitor's weakness and use it against them.

    b. **Flexibility**: Be responsive and adaptive to current conditions.

    c. **Leverage**: Find the strengths that give you momentum. One of the handiest strategic tools in modern business is the SWOT analysis because it helps a business uncover internal strengths and weaknesses as well as external opportunities and threats.

IX.   **The pivot and the hammer strategy:** Find the right attack-defence balance by utilising your assets to defend your market position whilst initiating an attack on another.

> Do not think of attack and defence as two separate things. An attack will be a

defence, and a defence must be an attack.[55]

Kazuzo Kudo, 9th dan

THINGS TO REMEMBER WHEN LAUNCHING YOUR PRODUCT

I.   Your value as a business is derived from your customers and key strategic partners.

II. Assumption is a dangerous monster that eats away potential success that can only be tamed and tapered by facts and good feedback from the market.

Ultimately, a company's value is just the sum of the decisions it makes and executes. [56]

Michael Mankins – HBR

Dr. Phineas Dube, a man I esteem greatly, often quoted Soren Kierkegaard, "Life is understood backwards and lived forwards." So with these words we can draw a lesson from history. In 218 B.C. the great general Hannibal from

---

[55] *Black Belt Magazine*, August 1968
[56] Steven Flinn, *Optimising Data-To-Learning-To-Action: The Modern Approach To Continuous Performance Improvement for Business* (Apress 2018)

Carthage (modern day Tunisia) decided to attack the great empire of Rome.[57] With an army of 20 thousand Carthaginian men Hannibal went up against the Roman army of 700 thousand infantry men and 70 thousand cavalry. With a small contingent he designed his attack to be swift, forceful and unpredictable. On war elephants he travelled through the Alps and attacked Rome from an unexpected direction. The Romans were caught off guard and lost significant territories to this ingenious strategy.

Entrepreneurs can take a page from Hannibal's strategy as they seek to launch a product and establish market share. We can make use of the limited resources we have, with a strong strategy and ingenuity to challenge for market share. Once the product is launched, the challenge is to sustain the project which often requires the one thing most entrepreneurs have a short supply of - resources. At this point there is the need to unleash the 300 Spartans, lessons of the bootstrapper!

[57] Polybius, *The Histories*, (OUP Oxford 2010)

Chapter 8   300 SPARTANS – ADEQUATE
CONCENTRATION OF RESOURCES

The story of the battle fought at Thermopylae by the famed King Leonidas, presents us with a lesson in courage and bravery in the face of an overwhelmingly large enemy or opposing force. [58]

With a force of 300 hundred men, Leonidas stood his ground against the massive armies of Xerxes. There are other stories that hold similar renown; Gideon and his 300 warriors and Garibalidi at Calatafimi in 1860. They provide the entrepreneur with insights into how to hold your own against a powerful competitor with minimal resources.

In reference to resources I would present a favoured phrase among most business planners in Japan, *hito* (people), *kane* (money) and *mono* (resources). How an entrepreneur adequately manages these 3 things determines how they grow and move forward. Resources

---

[58]   Terri   Doughterty,   *300   Heroes: The   Battle   of Thermopylae,*(Capstone 2009)

must be sufficiently focused to reduce the effects of warfare at the most expedient place and time to deliver and ensure decisive results.

The aim is to achieve the desired result in the shortest possible time and at the lowest possible cost. Adequate concentration of resources can ensure even the smallest army that is numerically disadvantaged can maximize and achieve desired results whilst minimizing human loss and wastage of material resources.

The 6th principle is dedicated to establishing an adequate concentration of resources. The entrepreneur must learn how to bootstrap and live within a very lean and tight budget for a certain period of time. Below are some keys to bootstrapping.

NINE KEYS TO BOOTSTRAPPING - DO MORE WITH LESS.

DELAYED GRATIFICATION OR PURCHASE.

One of the most important things in war is to travel with the resources and equipment necessary for the battle. Excess resources and gear must be left behind to ensure the efficient movement of forces and the effectiveness of the forces in question to achieve victory. A wise entrepreneur will delay as long as possible the purchase of noncritical and expensive assets or liabilities as these can often hinder the operations of the business.

FIND ANOTHER WAY TO GAIN ACCESS TO WHAT YOU WOULD OTHERWISE BUY OR LEASE.

Creativity and ingenuity work best when you find other ways around problems. It is often said, "Necessity is the mother of invention." One of the most interesting aspects of Roman conquests was their ability to travel with the necessary tools to build siege works and battlements using the resources on location.

Instead of travelling with large weapons, they travelled with a team of carpenters, blacksmiths and artisans to work on building their siege works on site. This allowed the Roman army to travel at great speed and to adequately instil the right degree of fear and anxiety to ensure victory.

UNDERSTAND THE DIFFERENCE BETWEEN WANTS AND NEEDS.

Business needs are critical to success; business wants could be strategic or outright perilous. You may **want** a car to increase deliveries but what you may really **need** is more stock and possibly software to help you improve stock turnover. The tide of the battle has been swung by the inability of generals to discern the difference between a need and a want. Failure to distinguish between the two can often be attributed to arrogance and pride which is the Achilles heel of any business and army.

CONDUCT YOUR BOOTSTRAPPING ACTIVITIES ETHICALLY AND WITH INTEGRITY.

There are legal and legitimate ways to cut corners and then there are illegal ways. Bootstrapping in its purest form is not about cheating or conning your way out of a situation but being ingeniously frugal.

One of the most important indicators of an innovation is the economic benefit and efficiency it delivers to the customer. The brilliance of the *corvus* was that it reduced the probability of the Romans losing battles at sea.

FOCUS ON GROWTH EXPENDITURE.

In any business, growth must be a key area of focus. As such resources should be dedicated to developing the necessary systems and frameworks to ensure that the business is positioned for growth. Importantly this speaks into differences between direct and fixed costs.

Growth is driven by the quality of production and distribution process. This is not to say that fixed costs should be neglected or ignored. Rather it is a matter of appreciating what determines success.

MANAGE COSTS.

Something as simple as a mobile phone bill can eat into your bottom line if not monitored and managed appropriately. Poorly amassing expenses may prove crippling at the end of any endeavour. One important aspect of cost management is delaying payments for a long as feasibly and morally possible. Whether it is large expenditures or things as small as paperclips.

> In the operations of war, where there are in the field a thousand swift chariots, as many heavy chariots, and a hundred thousand mail-clad soldiers, with provisions enough to carry them a thousand li [Chinese miles], the expenditure at home and at the front, including entertainment of guests, small items such as glue and paint, and

sums spent on chariots and armour, will reach the total of a thousand ounces of silver per day. Such is the cost of raising an army of 100,000 men. [59]

Sun Tzu

RESOURCEFULNESS, CREATIVITY, AND TENACITY ARE YOUR ONLY LIMITS.

There's more than one solution to a problem. The question is can you see it? One of the most important ingredients in war and business is ingenuity. Take for instance Hannibal's ambitious attack on Rome via the Alps riding on elephants in winter. This was something the Romans did not expect because they considered the Alps a natural defence and barrier.

Ingenuity points to the ability to do the unexpected or downright impossible. It wasn't just Hannibal's tactical brilliance that caught the Romans off guard but his skills in strategy and logistics; moving a large army through harsh conditions.

---

[59] Sun Tzu *The Art of War*, 35

REDUCE YOUR PERSONAL COST OF LIVING.

Lifestyle is one of the biggest pitfalls entrepreneurs face. When an entrepreneur gets the big deal, it is natural to want to flaunt the new found 'SUCCESS'. However a business cannot be deemed successful when it continues to be run from the founder's pocket.

Thus an important ingredient in effectively building a sustainable business is to ensure that an entrepreneur's living costs are aptly kept within appropriate limits and distinctly separated from the day to day running and performance of the business.

KNOW WHEN TO SHIFT GEARS OUT OF BOOTSTRAPPING.

Timing is everything and bootstrapping should not be the default but should rather be a strategic position aligned to prevailing circumstances. Once the opportunity lends itself to leverage more resources to grow, the entrepreneur must seize these moments with wisdom and tenacity.

FINAL THOUGHTS – LESSONS FROM THE HOT GATES.

I. **LAUNCH YOUR ATTACK WITHOUT DELAY**: Do not wait for the right timing or the right weather to face the competition or enemy. He who watches the clouds will not sow.[60] Leonidas and his 300 men knew that swiftness was of the utmost importance and that any delay would result in the advancing Persian army gaining more strategic ground.

II. **FOCUS ON CASH FLOW**: Use and sweat your resources wisely. As an entrepreneur, resources are scarce assets that need to be managed well. So too 300 men facing a horde of Persian forces. Though he was finally overrun Leonidas utilised his limited forces to great effect. There are 3 basic tenets of good cash flow management.

    a. Avoid credit sales, either get paid cash on delivery or create sufficient hype to get pre-orders

    b. Delay payments as long as possible.

    c. Keep your stock levels to a bare minimum.

---

[60] Ecclesiastes 11:4 New Kings James Version

Keep your cash for as long as possible and try and get paid quicker.

III. **NOTHING COMES CHEAP**: If it's cheap, it's suspect. There is always a price for everything. Every battle an entrepreneur faces in the market will cost something. The Spartans under Leonidas, knew that a stand against a larger force would've cost them their lives. Yet, they did not give away their position rashly or without a fight. Instead, it is said they gave Xerxes such a bad taste for battle.

IV. **LEVERAGE YOUR ASSETS**: Make good use of your assets, be it intangible networks and relationships or tangible assets like stocks and vehicles. Leonidas first and foremost knew his terrain well enough to know that the mountain pass called the Hot Gates was the best place to hold off a large army. Furthermore, his best asset as King of Sparta wasn't negotiation like Athens but battle and so he didn't hesitate to take on the larger Persian army using the skill at his disposal.

V. **BE PREPARED TO SACRIFICE:** Nothing is more imperative than for the founder to lay his/her life down for the cause. An established business requires time, effort, *hito, kane* and *mono* to succeed. In the face of total obliteration Leonidas did not shrink back from the challenge. So too Gideon and his 300 when faced with the growing reality that his force was diminished. Instead they both went forward boldly with the courage to take on what seemed to be an insurmountable challenge.[61]

[61] Terri Doughterty, *300 Heroes: The Battle of Thermopylae*

Chapter 9 ECONOMY OF FORCES –

THE DISRUPTOR

> "For which of you, desiring to build a tower, does
> not first count the cost, whether he has enough to
> complete it? Otherwise, when he has laid a
> foundation, and is not able to finish, all who see it
> begin to mock him saying, 'This man began to
> build and was not able to finish.' Or what king,
> going to encounter another king in war, will not sit
> down first and take counsel whether he is able with
> ten thousand men to meet him who comes against
> him with twenty thousand? And of not, while the
> other is far off, he sends an embassy and asks for
> terms of peace."[62]
>
> Jesus

Having spoken about taking on the market with limited
resources in Principle 6, the next principle is dedicated to
the economy of forces. The question will always be, how
can an entrepreneur take on the market share of a market
leader without causing any retaliation? Jesus simply says

---

[62] Luke 14:28 New International Version (NIV)

that someone must count the cost of what they are about to do. Can the market be taken with limited resources? Can a big company with millions be taken on by a smaller company with thousands or hundreds of thousands of dollars? The answer is probably not a direct yes or no and is subject to a number of factors.

> "He will win who knows how to handle both superior and inferior forces. [63]
>
> Sun Tzu

Throughout the early years of the second Punic wars between Carthage and Rome Hannibal inflicted some of the most crushing defeats on the Romans. One notable one was in the heart of Italy. Using the Roman's own territorial advantage, over-aggression and superiority against them, Hannibal ambushed the Roman army as they crossed a frozen river at the Battle of Cannae in 218

---

[63] Sun Tzu, *The Art Of War*, 15

BC.[64] What is important to note is that he achieved this with a significantly smaller force and limited resources.

YOUR TECHNE

The word culture originates from the Latin word *cultus*, which is the root word for cultivation. Efficiency is influenced as much by processes and systems as by people. Success is driven by the manner and how efficiently things are done. Technology is a word often associated with advanced devices like smartphones yet, at the core, technology speaks of the way things are done or the technique and approach applied to achieve a result.

One of the things that made Spartans a renowned force to be reckoned with was their approach to war. The Spartan citizen was raised with a military mind-set, war was infused into the Spartan way of life. Everything about the Spartan way of life conveyed the sense of war. The Spartans training philosophy called *Agoge* ensured that

---

[64] https://www.warhistoryonline.com/ancient-history/hannibal-couldnt-win-war-carthage.

Sparta developed a strong individual and team capable of defending the honour of Sparta.[65]

5 AGOGE *PRINCIPLES FOR EFFECTIVE VICTORY*

I.   **Learn stealth:** Like the Spartan a good entrepreneur needs to learn how to move without unnecessary detection. It is a skill that can be learned and acquired through the rigours of training. Stealth is a necessary approach to taking products to market. It is important for an entrepreneur not to draw unnecessary or unwanted attention from the competitor.

II. **Cultivate loyalty:** The effectiveness of any team comes down to the level of loyalty to the cause. The Spartan *Agoge* focused on raising young men into effective and unique individuals and made them loyal members of a team. Brand Loyalty begins with employee and team loyalty. If the business team is not committed to the vision it is

---

[65] Paula Cartledge, *Spartan Reflections*, (University of California Press 2003)

most likely they will not convince the customer to be loyal to the brand.

III. **Military training (Competence Development):** *Agoge* focused on equipping young men for battle using different techniques such as depriving them of food, clothing and sleep, the use of weapons and a solid fitness regimen.

IV. **Learn to Hunt:** Hunting was for the express purpose of learning self-sustenance through the exercise of pursuing, tracking trapping or killing. It also contributed to how the young Spartan men learned the skill of stealth and other modes of combat. With respect to business hunting, teaches the business team to prospect and secure customers for survival.

V. **Social interaction:** Importantly, the young Spartan men learned to operate within a team. Non-combat activities like singing, dancing and athletic games were designed to build strong social bonds. The cohesiveness of a team is a critical indicator of success. Cohesion is not built on the battlefield within a short space of time but over periods of time dedicated to knowing the person who sits on the desk next to you.

To achieve success, resources must be managed in such a way as to ensure victory, from the very conception of a business idea, to delivering the product to a customer. Therefore the process and the people must be raised, developed and equipped to achieve the sole objective of profitability through value creation.

CUSTOMERS BUILD AND GROW COMPANY RESOURCES.

The reason why large corporations are in business is because they deliver a certain level of value consistently. The question for the entrepreneur is simply that; can he or she find customers in the market that welcome the value delivered by their business? Customers determine the rise and fall of any business.

Businesses may have great products and solutions but, if they are not bought it means the business has no going concern. In war, victory is often determined by the object of war and the size of army necessary to force the enemy to retreat or give up territory. Having a customer centric business is much like having an army bent on and motivated by victory. The object and heart of that army is to be victorious in their endeavours. Hence, at the core of any business are the efforts and energy expended to acquire customers.

THERE ARE SMALL MARKETS THE BIG PLAYERS ARE NOT INTERESTED IN?

In any given industry, there are opportunities that exist unless of course the market is in the late stages of maturity. But even in late stages of maturity there lies an opportunity for innovation. Hence the entrepreneur has the express prospect to challenge for market share without expending a lot of resources challenging the big players. This means developing a unique appreciation of the market or industry they are entering.

For instance, an entrepreneur must understand the visible and invisible barriers to entry. An appreciation of this allows an entrepreneur to prepare for the fight ahead. Targeting unwanted markets is a chance to deliver value and to initiate value chain reconfiguration or niching as a growth strategy. The focus when engaging in value chain reconfiguration would be to minimize the effort and cost incurred when delivering a service. Often the reason a large corporate isn't interested in the specific market could be the low margins, cost of a transaction, a convoluted process or the degree of risk. Therefore the opportunity would be to create an innovation that solves one or all of the abovementioned challenges.

IF IT'S NOT THERE THEN SOMETIMES IT'S REALLY NOT THERE?

Entrepreneurs are sometimes plagued with the illusion that they have a product that can take the market by storm. Entrepreneurs may have developed a product based on a generic technology that anyone can use e.g. open source software or recipes downloaded from the internet.

It is upon this illusion that they build a business, believing that they have enough competitive advantage to blow an incumbent out of the water. Building on a weak foundation is similar to 'not having' a business at all, because it results in the same outcome; failure. To be competitive means either delivering what the competitor cannot deliver or surpassing the competitor's offer. By all intents and purposes this means building something that is unique and appealing to the customer.

STRENGTHS DEFINE WEAKNESSES

In Chapter Five, I mentioned the six pillars of the future and mentioned that there's one called the disowned future. Many businesses are built on strengths alone. It is a very logical thing to do, as such no one would build on their weakness as that is tantamount to failure. Yet, internal weaknesses are often the key threats that destroy a business. Any sane competitor attacks a business' weaknesses.

Hence internal weaknesses are not things to be ignored rather, they ought to be understood and appreciated as areas that a business can strengthen or mitigate in the face of a threat. As an entrepreneur discovers their strengths it must follow that their inherent weaknesses in the business become apparent.

These weaknesses serve to highlight where threats could come from. One such example is the Phoenician army whose strength was seafaring but their weakness was in combat.

By building the *corvus* the Romans gained strength over their internal naval weaknesses and an advantage against their enemy in spite of the notable Phoenician nautical agility. For the Phoenicians the cost of ignoring their weakness was losing their territory and ultimately the war.

I.   How can you use your opportunities to overcome the weaknesses you recognize in your business?

II. How can you minimize your weaknesses to avoid threats and predatory attacks from your competitors?

SUPPLY MAY NOT ALWAYS EQUAL DEMAND

When an entrepreneur develops a product or offers a service, it will not always follow that customers will come rushing in to purchase. An express appreciation of this reality helps an entrepreneur develop the supporting systems required to court the interest of the targeted customers.

Simply put, customers need to know that the product exists. Once customers have bought the product they need further support in, using the product or buying it again. Demand is driven by derived experiences. Customers consume based on the benefits and experiences they garner from a product or service.

THE NINE DOS OF EFFECTIVE UTILISATION

i. **DO SOMETHING RIGHT OR BETTER:** instead of focusing on growth for the sake of growth, focus on improving processes that make you more competitive.

ii. **BE AN AGGREGATOR:** manage your supply chain hierarchy.

iii. **AIM FOR 80-85% PRODUCTION CAPACITY:** reduce production costs via learning, knowledge and experience. Focus on building local skills or outsource cheaper international skills.

iv. **PRODUCE MOST OF PRODUCT OR CONTROL THE CORE INNOVATION:** develop a strong profit centre by managing your variable costs.

v. **FOCUS ON ADDRESSING KEY COMPONENT CHALLENGES**: What made the corvus an amazing innovation is, it focused on solving the Roman army's challenges at sea. Work on improving the cost of the most expensive or complicated component.

vi. **MASTER INTEGRATION**: reduce the power of suppliers by building stronger relationships and focus on improving productivity.

vii. **UNDERSTAND YOUR COST STRUCTURE**: what makes sense? Manage and implement customer feedback, develop systems to enhance production management and spur or drive innovation especially process and business model.

viii. **ATTACK THE MARKET ON THREE FRONTS**: there are three dimensions of profit, value, price and cost.

ix. **MARKET VALUE**: Are people buying? Why are they buying? Why are they not buying?

So can the entrepreneur take on the big business?

The answer lies in what Jesus said, "For which of you, desiring to build a tower, does not first count the cost, whether he has enough to complete it?"[66]

Take counsel

An entrepreneur must be open to advice from reliable and competent counsellors. One of the hallmarks of great generals was that they had men around them that provided wise counsel in matters of war. Counsel also points to the ability to leverage knowledge and experience from team members and key partners.

As an example adequate supplier information helps to ascertain the length of time it will take to be profitable or to break even. Furthermore, good and wise counsel always points out weaknesses in the value proposition.

Planning

An entrepreneur should consider the future and potential outcomes. Planning means counting the cost; inadequate planning always leads to failure. A poorly

---

[66] Luke 14:28 New International Version (NIV)

planned war is an expensive one in so many respects. An infamous and dismally planned war was the one fought by King Pyrrhus.

Though he won the battle it came at such a great cost that he counted it as a defeat and today costly victories are known as Pyrrhic victories. Planning saves an entrepreneur from making costly decisions in the field of battle by simulating them from a secure base.

DEVELOP STRATEGY

Strategy helps to shape the direction and course of action an entrepreneur needs to take. Strategy implies an appreciation of the cost and how to successfully overcome cost to achieve profit. Strategy helps the entrepreneur unfurl the *desired* future for the business, and helps to prevent and mitigate an *undesirable or calamitous one.*

VISION

An entrepreneur must consider whether they are in for the long haul. A business is a going concern existing in a dynamic environment. So with this in consideration, an entrepreneur can proceed to step out of their secure base and face the market leader in possession of millions of dollars and a large chunk of the market share with an idea, a few hundred dollars and tons of optimism and passion. Importantly with answers to the following questions:

I.   What is your intended desire for the future?

II.   What are the facts relating to what you see?

III. What are the problems and potential threats and challenges you may face?

IV.   How many solutions can you uncover for the problems you discover?

V.   As you examine and re-examine all possible solutions, which one is the best and most workable option?

TERMS OF PEACE

A profound concept that might serve as a means not only to save a small business from the keen interest and intent of a larger enemy, is establishing terms of peace. The idea of peace is central to the reason people fight or avert war. Jesus points out the idea of negotiating terms of peace, he points out to an important tactical element of war; a win-win situation.

The master strategist must find ways of achieving his objective without expending too many resources. The combination of a niche and value reconfiguration strategy can create opportunities to negotiate 'peace' with a market leader.

If an entrepreneur can find a unique benefit for the market leader this is the springboard for successfully redirecting the attention of market leader. Ideally, an entrepreneur must think of ways not to be perceived as a threat.

It was the priest who met Alexander the Great as he approached Jerusalem, who inspired him to take on the known world. Establishing peaceful terms is a diversionary tactic that achieves your core objective, victory.

When the armies of Rome sought to advance the *Pax Romana* concept further south after invading Egypt they met a powerful Kushite/Nubian kingdom under the leadership of a female queen called

Candace *Amanirenas*.[67] After a fearsome battle led by this great female general the Romans were brought to the negotiating table.

The representatives of Candace brought a token from their queen for Augustus in the form of a bundle of golden arrows and a message from the queen purportedly stating that "The Candace sends you these arrows. If you want peace, they are a token of her friendship and warmth. If you want war, you are going to need them."

The peace agreement reflects the influence and power of Candace as she left with her territory intact and without the need to pay Roman taxes. Whilst the Roman Empire expanded elsewhere the Barawa kingdom lived on for 300 years.

> In respect of the military method, we have, firstly measurement, secondly estimation of quantity, thirdly calculation, fourthly, balancing of chances and fifthly, victory.[68]

---

[67] Derek A. Welby, *The Kingdom of Kush: The Naptan and Meroitic Empires* (British Musuem Press 2002)
[68] Sun Tzu, *The Art of War*, 23

FIVE KEYS OF DISRUPTION

5 keys of disruption below are derived from Sun Tzu's military method relate to the adventure of business and enterprise.[69]

I. **Measure**: Decide what is required to achieve victory by prospection, contemplation and knowledge.

II. **Estimate**: Guesstimate the resources required to successfully achieve the perceived objectives.

III. **Calculate**: Meticulously work out the actual costs of your endeavour.

IV. **Determine**: Work out your chances of success.

V. **Conquer**: Act with the sole intent to be victorious.

---

[69] Ibid,39

Chapter 10 THE ELEMENT OF SURPRISE (STEALTH ATTACK)

> One of the strongest weapons of offensive warfare
> is the surprise attack. The closer we come to it,
> the more fortunate we shall be.[70]
>
> Carl von Clausewitz

Industries and markets will always constitute those that have and those that don't have. There, will always be someone who supplies and someone who demands. In business, there will always be the market leader who possesses a significant proportion of the market, a challenger who is attempting to capture a portion of the market, and a new entrant who is simply inspired to set up shop and get a part of the market.

All entrepreneurs successful or otherwise at some point started off as new entrants or passionate novices eager to break into the market. The success of an early stage venture is highly dependent on how much attention it

---

[70] Carl von Clausewitz, *Principles of War*,(Courier Corporation 2012)

draws from the market leader and some of the most prominent challengers. Successful attempts to prize market share from a competitor can result from effectively attacking the market when it is least expected.

The Romans never expected that Hannibal would attack Rome. The French never expected the fighting women of Dahomey to attack by night. The key to a surprise attack is the ability to secretly position the business for a particular target audience with unclear advantages.

The key to this is to attack the market from an unexpected position. Both Hannibal and the women of Dahomey used the surprise attack to full effect by striking the enemy when it was least prepared.

The impenetrability of the Macedonian phalanx was broken when the Romans attacked them from the side whilst maintaining a frontal position. This exposed the rigidity and immobility of the phalanx and forced the Macedonians to break it.[71] A market may have high barriers of entry or a company with a very dominant

---

[71] Richard A. Billows, *Kings and Colonists: Aspects of Macedonian Imperialism*, (Brill 1995),16

product that seems to make the particular market impenetrable.

Yet, in essence every business has a weakness, and the strength of a good stealth attack is to find and exploit the weakness; attack under the cover of night from the side or rearguard. From the side implies approaching the less appreciated customers within the market who tend to feel neglected and are likely to switch easily when offered better customer experience.

Attacking from the rearguard points to attacking the competitor's complacency by confronting long standing clients who no longer garner any value from the competitor's offering. These may be long serving customers who the competitor ignores as a result of a long standing relationship.

> He will win who, prepared himself, waits to take
> the enemy unprepared.[72]
>
> Sun Tzu

---

[72] Sun Tzu, *The Art of War*, 44

The 8th principle of the Catapult Effect is centred on one of the most important principles of war that may determine the success or failure of a campaign. It is imperative that a small business maintain the element of surprise. The surprise attack has caught many an enemy unaware and unprepared.

The most famous of these stories is the attack of Troy using a horse that was presented as a gift but turned out to be the curse of defeat. Yet, I will focus this chapter on the story of a group of famous fighting women truly recognized as the Amazonians of history; the fighting women of Dahomey.

CUSTOMERS

Customers are a key ingredient in business. With no customers to purchase your product or service, there is no business. The astute entrepreneur will identify at least two types of customers that the incumbent either cannot see or completely refuse to see.

SERVE THE UNWANTED OR UNSATISFIED CUSTOMER

Every industry has that customer no one really wants to deal with. They may be difficult, of lesser value and importance to the incumbent or downright inconsequential. As a challenger or entrant this customer represents a great opportunity for your business to deliver value whilst under the radar.

FIND THE UNKNOWN OR NEW CUSTOMER

Innovation is the buzzword in most industries today, as they face stagnation and life cycle maturity. Innovation is generally a costly venture in most industries especially when it is the radical innovation of a product or solution. But there are other areas of innovation that are not as costly. As an entrepreneur observation is a strong asset that helps to find the unknown customer.

Over the years Africa's rural unbanked money went by unknown and unappreciated. Suddenly, thanks to Mpesa in Kenya everyone is clamouring for their money.[73] An

---

[73] M-Pesa is a mobile phone-based money transfer, financing and micro-financing service, launched in 2007 by Vodafone for Safaricom and Vodacom, the largest mobile network operators in Kenya and Tanzania. https://en.wikipedia.org/wiki/M-Pesa

entrepreneur can be the first one to see and serve the unknown and unwanted and thus develops solid first mover advantage in an industry.

War history is riddled with examples of how whilst two opposing enemies were fighting a 3rd force was emerging by accumulating unwanted territories. By such tactics the Roman Empire grew from a small city of 310,000 inhabitants to an empire amid the military and economic might of the Carthaginians, Macedonians and Gauls by taking the Italian peninsula. As the masses fight for the big corporate or high net worth individual, your business could be looking for the small pebble that starts an avalanche of profitability.

DISRUPTION

For every industry there are known and accepted ways of doing things, often called benchmarks. As important as these standards may be, they are vulnerable to changes in the environment. A particular way of doing things could change as a result of changes in customer preferences or changes in government policy for instance. An entrepreneur can find or unlock the next wave of change.

For instance though the market may be fixated on the automated teller machine (ATM) the entrepreneur could venture into secure web based payment solutions for the emerging generation.

Where the hospitality industry is dominated by expensive holiday packages in hotels, a hospitality and travel business could focus on niche and customized solutions for families. Shaka the Zulu represents the true power of disruption.

At a time when different tribes had an accepted way of fighting and certain rules of engagement Shaka introduced a new way. Instead of throwing spears back and forth, Shaka designed a short fighting spear called the *assegai*.[74]

Disruption is strongly linked to innovation. Entrepreneurs are those that seek to challenge the market status quo through innovative solutions that not only change how business is done but drive the markets forward.

---

[74] Dan Wylie, Shaka (JacanMedia2011) 55

TIMING

Stealth implies knowing when to attack. Sun Tzu recommends that one of the essentials for victory is knowing when to fight and knowing when not to. Furthermore, he talks about what to do in light of the size of an army. In business it is imperative to know when to strike. As the mantra often goes; the first one to make a move often wins but sometimes it is the one who delays or strikes when least expected who comes out victorious.

The Macedonians were renowned for their *hoplite phalanx* which was an impenetrable infantry formation that would advance them to victory. In a famous battle with the Romans the famed Macedonian phalanx was broken down by a simple decoy.

Realizing that the phalanx was hard to break down from the front the Romans divided their armies into two forces. When the Macedonians attacked as usual they did not realize that there was another force of Romans that was going to attack from the rear. This exposed a weakness of the phalanx; the inability to turn without breaking the formation. The impenetrable phalanx was broken.[75]

In business an entrepreneur can challenge a more prominent business by devising the right strategy of attack or simply put, finding the incumbent's weakness.

> When able to attack, we must seem unable; when using our forces, we must seem inactive; when we are near, we must make the enemy believe we are far away; when far away, we must make him believe we are near.[76]
>
> Sun Tzu

Though it seems obvious that an enemy is more likely to attack at night, the story of the fighting women of Dahomey presents a profound lesson in war on the tactical brilliance of a surprise attack. The fighting women of Dahomey were extremely successful in their battles because they mastered the art of stealthily attacking at night. Their success in battle was down to timing and

---

[75] Richard A. Billows, *Kings and Colonists: Aspects of Macedonian Imperialism*,16
[76] Sun Tzu, *The Art of War*

143

disruption. The timing and nature of their attacks often caught their enemies off guard.[77]

I strongly believe that most men succumbed in battle because they underestimated the fighting and strategic abilities of these women. When these men saw that the principal fighting force of Dahomey were but women they made the wrong assumption that is aptly captured by Sun Tzu. The assumption that the women did not have the ability to attack much less do so at night was their greatest pitfall.

SMOKE SCREEN

Red bull offers us a lesson in diversion. By not competing directly with Coca Cola and Pepsi, they were able to enter the cola market without drawing any serious attention to themselves. On the other hand in my country RC Cola drew unnecessary attention from a company that had a monopoly on the soft drink market. Red Bull

---

[77] Stanley B. Alpern, *Amazons of Black Sparta: The Women Warriors of Dahomey*, (NYU Press 2011)

was racing right next to Coca Cola and Pepsi Cola but never seemed or looked like a direct competitor.

RISK OF FAILURE

When a big company fails the losses are glaring and often insurmountable. This is because they have to manage their image and deal with more stakeholders; there are greater implications on the bottom-line. An emerging entrepreneur can risk more with a lower cost. Hence, an entrepreneur can go where no other business in the industry has gone before *(the race for space)*.

Risk is a big stumbling block for big companies but it can be a stepping stone for the budding entrepreneur. In the words of Thomas Carlyle the famous Scottish writer, "A block of granite in the pathway of the weak is an obstacle but in the pathway of the strong it is a stepping stone."[78] The entrepreneur should be strong where the big corporate is 'weak and weary' of seizing emerging opportunities.

---

[78] John Mason, *Believe You Can, The Power of A Positive Attitude*, (Revell 2010)

Six elements of Market Penetration

Finally, some points to reflect on adapted from Clayton Christenson from his book the Innovator's Dilemma,

I. **PLAN FOR FAILURE**: Nothing will work the first time. If at first you don't succeed dust yourself up and try again. Strategy is as much about success as it is about preparing for pitfalls and obstacles along the way. One of the most important questions to ask within a planning session is, "What if..." building a premise that anticipates both success and failure points to good strategic planning. The successful generals in battle prepared and anticipated failure by creating alternative scenarios. The study of scenarios is essentially looking at the likelihood of the plan failing.

II. **DON'T COUNT ON BREAKTHROUGHS**: Find use for what you have: one disastrous aspect of good and well managed businesses is the desire for miraculous, serendipitous or unplanned breakthroughs. Rather, look at different ways to package existing technologies in different and unique architectures for new applications.

III. **FIND THE SIMPLER AND CHEAPER SOLUTION:** This may not have very high margins. Find the point of least resistance or the shortest path to achieve your ends.

IV. **COMMERCIALIZE** your product in emerging or insignificant or unwanted industries. What made mobile banking a revolutionary idea is it targeted places and people that traditional banks in Africa were not interested in.

V. **MARKETS THAT DON'T EXIST CANNOT BE ANALYSED:** Find the markets that do not exist and create them. The whole concept of market space points to having the ability to foresee emergent opportunities. The are 4 focal points to consider

a. **INVESTMENT FOCUS:** invest time, money and resources in the areas that will create a competitive edge.

b. **GROWTH FOCUS:** harness and design emergent opportunities that will lead to growth and development.

c. **MARKET FOCUS:** focus on creating value and generating rich experiences for the customer.

d. **RISK FOCUS:** create the necessary countermeasures and strategies to mitigate the effects of risk.

VI. **DEPEND ON CUSTOMERS FOR RESOURCES**: The best way to resource your business is to find the right customers that will buy your product. Validation of a concept is measured by the feedback generated by a customer's decision to purchase. The greatest investment a business can make is to deliver value that a customer will pay for.

As soon the business finds a position to leverage, entrepreneurs can fully experience the quantum leap that leads towards profitability. Yet, what becomes apparent is that the enemy or your competitor won't be surprised for long thus it becomes imperative to make decisions and act fast.

ENGAGE IN STRATEGIC CONFLICT

The true power of the stealth attack is to use fast and effective decision making to keep competitors and rivals off balance so as to achieve competitive outcomes. This is achieved through making the right strategic investments, controlling information and sending the right signals at the right time.

Stealth attacks create a pivot that shifts the tide of battle and balance of power to achieve success, in most cases with very little resistance. Factors contributing to surprise include;

I.   Speed in decision-making,
II.   Information sharing, and
III. Force movement;
IV.   Effective intelligence;
V.   Ploy or Decoy;
VI.   Application of unexpected combat power;
VII. Variations in tactics and methods of operation.

These 7 elements are captured in the story of Amanirenas the queen of the Meriotic or Kushite kingdom which was situated in presented day Sudan and Egypt. When the

Romans attacked and overthrew Egypt, it was almost obvious that the southern Kushite kingdom would be next. Knowing this, Amanirenas made a decision to attack the Roman garrisons situated in southern Egypt in Syene and Philiae. Together with her son Akinidad they managed to defeat the Roman forces there. Not only was this a decisive act it had all the hallmarks of a good surprise attack.[79]

---

[79] Kevin Shillington, *History of Africa* (Macmillan International Higher Education, 2012)

Chapter 11 MOBILITY AND FLEXIBILITY

An interesting fact is that some wars have been fought and won by an army with few men. One such battle I was told about is the Battle of Ikela where a small group of about 120 Zimbabwean commandos held off and defeated a full battalion of rebels in the Democratic Republic of Congo.

They won the battle because they made quick decisions and expedited their implementation. It is the same with modern day business and entrepreneurship. Charles Handy predicted the present day age to be the Age of Unreason, because instability and change would be the buzzwords of management and leadership.[80] The 9th principle of the Catapult Effect addresses these challenges.

> Unless important advantages are to be gained from hesitation, it is necessary to set to work at once. By this speed a hundred enemy measures are nipped in the bud and public opinion is won

---

[80] Charles Handy, *The Age of Unreason*, (Random House 2012)

rapidly. Surprise plays a much greater role in strategy than in tactics. It is most the most important element in victory. Napoleon, Frederick II, Gustavus Adolphus, Caesar, Hannibal and Alexander owe the brightest rays of their fame to their swiftness.[81]

Claus von Clausewitz

The fundamental issue in mobility and flexibility is to gain advantage through swift decision making. As with war, success in business is reliant on the element of surprise. Doing the unexpected in business or causing disruption is the preserve of great strategic thinkers. The Greek phalanx is renowned throughout history for its effectiveness in the heat of battle as captured by the movie 300 Spartans.

Nonetheless it had one fundamental weakness; it was rigid especially when the Greeks used their long spears. And this was duly exposed by a mobile and agile Roman general who decided to split his force and attack a Greek phalanx from different directions. The important highlight for entrepreneurs is effectively adapting to changes in the

---

[81] Carl von Clausewitz, *Principles of War*

market. Von Clausewitz says "... that it is the most important element of victory."[82] To be truly victorious in business the entrepreneur must have the capacity to swiftly counteract the activities of competitors by having a strategy that combines a long term perspective with flexible short term decisions.

> Change—anticipating it, preparing for it, initiating it—is a crucial part of what leadership is all about. And leadership is not getting any easier, not with change coming faster all the time, accelerated by technology that instantly disseminates new information and ideas around the globe. To be successful in riding the wild, unpredictable waves of change, organizations today must be smoothly agile—able to adjust quickly to abrupt shifts in the marketplace, and able to move quickly to exploit suddenly emerging business opportunities.[83]

> Steven A. Ballmer - CEO, Microsoft Corporation

There are a few things we can draw from Steven Ballmer.

---

[82] Ibid
[83] Clifford Geertz, *The Interpretation of Cultures*, (Basic Books 2017)

CHANGE

We are living in a time of rapid and unpredictable change. In just a week Japan experienced three disasters that significantly affected the livelihood of its people.

Change is inevitable whether it is slow and evolutionary, systematic and planned or rapid, unstable and revolutionary. Of note Steven Ballmer states that change is coming faster all the time and it is accelerated by technology.

It almost seems the Butterfly Effect concept has become a significant part of our daily lives. What happens in a small town in Japan now affects business in Zimbabwe. In the 20th Century or earlier this would never have been considered plausible yet, today this is the order of the day.

THE API FOR SUCCESSFUL CHANGE MANAGEMENT

ANTICIPATING IT: The CEO of Samsung once said, "The future is not meant to be predicted but created." Anticipating the future is one critical skill attributable to the strategist.

As Pericles said, "Future ages will wonder at us as present ages wonder at us now." When the Greeks developed democracy, constitutions and the concept of the republic, it is most likely that they saw and anticipated its future impact. It was later applied by the Romans and eventually became the cornerstone of modern society.

PREPARING FOR IT: Creating the future means making the necessary plans for tomorrow today. It is imperative that leaders and managers prepare their teams and businesses for what's about to come.

Change is inevitable; be it markets, customer preferences, technology, learning approaches and ultimately people themselves are on a constant trajectory of change, growing, developing and morphing over time.

What separates good companies from great companies is the ability to prepare for the future. Vegetius a Roman philosopher once said, "He who desires peace must prepare for war."[84] The entrepreneur who desires incontestable market positions must be prepared for

---

[84] Flavius Vegetius Renatus, Karl Lang, *Epitoma Rei Militaris* (CHIZINE PUBN,2018)

attacks from strong competition. The great empires were built by men and women who were prepared for war founded on a desire for peace.

INITIATING IT: We can deduce that the downfall of many great empires and businesses, was due to their greatness and success. The decline of Rome, Greece and similarly some great businesses was as a result of their achievements and what they had done i.e. they were living in the past. They failed to see the need to change and hence drifted 'successfully' into antiquity.

Entrepreneurs are often pointed out to be people who take risks and show initiative. This means they have the capacity to recognize, harness and implement opportunity. To successfully respond to change requires proactive engagement with the environment as a catalyst and initiator.

LEADERSHIP

The above three aspects of change have become critical factors in leading and managing a business. It's no longer enough to apply business models and frameworks in light of a stable and predictable trend. The trend now is being unpredictable. Ideas are being disseminated faster, information is now accessible at just the click of a button and it would seem time is moving much faster. The ability to influence and shape direction quickly and accurately is of paramount importance.

> We can surprise the opponent by marching to the side or to the rear and suddenly advancing again. Or should we be far from the enemy, we can through unusual energy and activity arrive faster than he expect us.[85]
>
> Claus von Clausewitz

Ancient war was fought over a long period of time. Success in these drawn out wars was determined by the tactical ability of the general to deal with changing situations in battle. Leadership can easily be measured by the ability of a leader to handle change especially when it is unexpected.

In ancient Greece a general was not appointed based on lineage or class but on their ability on the battleground. A

---

[85] Carl von Clausewitz, *Principles of War*

man was appointed to lead if he showed great acts of bravery on the battlefield; he had to be a man who the soldiers would follow to the death.

Hannibal was one such notable and charismatic leader who was able to lead an army made of different nationalities and tribes. He not only slept among the ordinary soldiers, a sign of trust and integrity, but he also experienced the hardships that ordinary soldiers faced such as hunger when supplies ran low.

AGILITY

I love Standard Bank South Africa's strap line, "Moving Forward." There is great value in understanding what this means strategically in volatile and unpredictable times. It's one thing to try and tackle the future with the same weapons of the past or to concert and concentrate all your forces to face an invisible foe.

It is another to appreciate change and embrace the future with adequate planning and decision making combined with strategic action. To be propelled into a future of profitability and success organizations and entrepreneurs alike must be agile. To achieve this entrepreneurs must engage in the following:

FAST DECISION MAKING

Unless important advantages are to be gained from hesitation, it is necessary to set to work at once.[86]

Claus von Clausewitz

There is nothing more important in business or war than rapid and effective decision making. The whole concept of agility points to the ability to think fast in the midst of battle. Plans become redundant in the midst of changing situations in the market. Yet, planning becomes the pearl of the wise entrepreneur.

The story is told of a Roman general who was struggling to break down a large army of Macedonians whose phalanx seemed impenetrable. The plan he had put in place was not working and he was losing a lot of men. In the face of defeat the general divided his force and decided to attack the phalanx from different directions.

---

[86] Carl von Clausewitz, *Principles of War*

This was an innovative solution because it uncovered the one weakness the phalanx had; poor mobility. Once in formation it was difficult for the phalanx to change direction without breaking apart and reforming. The Roman general's ability to act and think fast, changed the course of the battle and ironically exposed the lack of agility in the Macedonian army.

UNDERSTANDING THE MARKET

Customer needs are shifting. More than 20 years ago a mobile phone was a trendy device that very few people needed. Today it is a necessity. A few years ago small mobile phones were in great demand but today the larger the smartphone the better.

Some businesses have failed because they didn't anticipate, prepare and initiate a shift towards the smartphone. To survive businesses must understand customer preferences and respond accordingly.

Empires have risen and fallen on this premise. Great empires like Babylon, Greece, Egypt, Munhumutapa and so forth have all fallen on the basis of their inability to adapt to the changes in their environment. The Greek empire was renowned for its mighty phalanx with long spears however they failed to anticipate and counter the emergence of the Romans' large shields and short fighting swords for close combat.

Understanding the market means being open to new experiences and change. Customer preferences are like shifting sands in the desert hence the prudent entrepreneur is one who willingly takes such shifts in stride. Shaka Zulu achieved great renown and success by accepting change.

During the life and times of Shaka, wars were fought with long javelins that were thrown back and forth by opposing armies. Enemies would hurl insults and spears at each other with the hope of slowly killing off the other army with the accuracy of their throws. Shaka changed the playing field when he designed a short spear the *assegai*.

> Value migrates from outmoded business designs to ones that are better able to satisfy customers' most important priorities.[87]

---

[87] Adrian Slywotzky, *The Profit Zone: How Strategic Business Design Will Lead You To Tomorrow's Profits*, (Crown Publishing Group 2007)

Adrian Slywotzky

There are particular approaches and customs in the market place that have an appearance of efficiency that easily become redundant when confronted by innovation or reconfiguration.

CREATING NEW MARKETS

Consider for a moment what will property development be like in 2040? For many of us it is unforeseeable but to some it is an emergent reality that can be shaped. Michell Zappa a futurist predicted a hybrid mix of ecology and architecture appropriately named archologies as the way cities will be built.

At present, there are many projects around the world looking to build sustainable 'SMART' cities. Property development is in for exciting change. Technology companies like Samsung are creating appliances that are greener and more interactive i.e. 'SMARTER'.

> Today's successful business leaders will be those who are most flexible of mind. They will have the ability to embrace new ideas and routinely

challenge old ones. They will be alert to learning from others and quickly adapt from the best.[88]

Tom Peters

The battle ground and landscape is changing and some armies are responding to this. One critical aspect of this is decision making and the processes that make organizations and businesses leaner and more responsive to subtle shifts in the environment. The leaders and entrepreneurs who have flexibility of mind. No matter how beautiful business plans look, it all boils down to how the plans are implemented. This points to the continuous process of planning and adapting to changing situations with the panache of a seasoned general.

> In respect of the military method, we have, firstly measurement, secondly estimation of quantity, thirdly calculation, fourthly, balancing of chances and fifthly, victory.[89]

Sun Tzu

---

[88] Tom Peters, *Thriving On Chaos: Handbook for a Management Revolution*, (HarperCollins 1988)

[89] Sun Tzu, *The Art of War*

Chapter 12 THE POWER OF

COLLABORATION

Though mobility and flexibility are necessary they are not sufficient to catapult your business into the next phase of growth. Importantly, every army needs to operate as a team. Collaboration involves key stakeholders like government and customers and can also come from your closest and fiercest competitors.

Strategic cooperation/alliance can be defined as an agreement between two or more independent companies which join individual capabilities and/or resources to pursue joint activities with the purpose to increase and maintain competitive advantages of co-operators across time.

When faced with an insurmountable barrier in business or a very powerful incumbent, collaboration is a useful tool to get around challenges. In the history of war collaboration has often been viewed as a weakness or as negative action with terms like traitor and sell-out being used. But viewed from the enemy's viewpoint, collaboration is a powerful strategy. It is the ability, to harness the potential of your environment or the incumbent's market share to your advantage.

The best example in war that captures the essence and value of collaboration are the Hellenic, Peloponnesian and Delian Leagues. To ward of the Persian onslaught Greece's independent states had to unite.

As smaller states and units the outcome of battle was obvious because the Persians had a larger and better resourced army. Yet, as a unified front the Greek city states were able to repel the Persians. The leagues and alliances served both as a method of attack and defence against attack.

In business this means finding the partners and stakeholders that enlarge your resource base and make you look larger and stronger than you were before. Collaboration means that the unique skills and resources of different stakeholders can be used to take on the market. One of the key highlights of the Delian League is that it brought together the resources and skills of smaller and larger states within Greece together. The Hellenic league also included the military might of the Spartans.

What these collaborations and alliances reveal is that there are elements that may be lacking in your business that exist in another smaller business in the market. Rather, than waste time slowly chipping away at the incumbent in a war of attrition with limited success, collaboration can be a powerful tool to catalyse acceleration and achieve traction.

Collaboration can also be a matter of finding the customer base the incumbent is disinterested in and working closely with that company or target audience to build a strong product that meets and satisfies the customer's needs. This is a niche strategy that strives to make the customer your collaborator, thus providing you with information and insights into what they value.

Collaboration could also look at an inefficient point in the value chain and market that can be considered a point of weakness. This could be a supplier frustrated by delayed payments or challenger in the market with poor processes. Such inefficiencies are an opportunity to reconfigure the value chain. Reconfiguration can often be associated and linked to innovation.

Lastly, collaboration points to the ability to create an innovation that leverages the strength of key stakeholders, customers, government, or suppliers. The whole concept of the Catapult Effect is hinged on the power of leverage, by unlocking the assets that give your business the momentum to trigger significant growth.

THREE ELEMENTS OF COLLABORATION

Collaboration brings significant fluidity in the decision process when a large or small group of people from different backgrounds agree on a particular direction faster than normal. Wars have been won by one decisive shift that was agreeable to everybody in spite of the possible risk involved. There are key aspects necessary for effective and fruitful collaboration. There are 3 key ingredients to successful collaboration namely, knowledge, technology and skills.

SHARING KNOWLEDGE AND INFORMATION - SHAPING OF IDEAS AND STRATEGY

Knowledge sharing is a critical ingredient in collaboration and serves as the bedrock for successful collaborations. The Spartans knowledge of the terrain specifically the Hot Gates was just as important as the Athenians knowledge and skill as seafarers. Without access to knowledge the wars against the Persians would certainly have been lost. From a business viewpoint knowledge sharing could be the difference between significant profits and failed entry into the market.

There are different forms of knowledge that can be uncovered in a business. There are 3 very important ones that determine whether a business can move forward with the pace and effectiveness necessary to achieve profit.

I.   **TACIT KNOWLEDGE:** This is unique knowledge and skill often hidden in individuals and almost applied subconsciously within the business. It is not recorded or shared explicitly with other people.

II. **EXPLICIT KNOWLEDGE:** This is knowledge that is shared with all and is very clear to every team member. The appropriate word for this knowledge is codification i.e. it is engrained in the fabric of the organisation's culture.

III. **EXECUTABLE KNOWLEDGE**: This is knowledge that can be utilised and implemented frequently and repeatedly achieving the same or improved results.

Of constituents, comrades and confidantes - what you share with whom.

It is significantly more important to share knowledge with the right people. War history is littered with turning points that changed the outcome of a battle because strategic information was shared with the wrong person. In some cases it was a betrayal of trust, in other cases it was simply giving out too much or sensitive information unnecessarily. Information in any business should therefore be strategically managed.

Knowledge sharing in a collaborative context in business can happen in 3 different ways:

I. **CONSTITUENTS**: This generally comprises a wide range of stakeholders i.e. customers, competitors, government bodies etc.

a. In terms of information it is imperative that an entrepreneur never share the most intimate details of their business with broad constituents. It is sufficient for them to know of your existence and to acknowledge what you have to offer.
b. It is also important that this group of collaborators have access to a constant stream and flow of general information relating to the business.
c. Jack Ma once said, "Love the government but don't get married to it." This is the best way to express the value of constituents and their limits and bounds. Though constituents are important they should never possess critical and sensitive information about your business.[90]

II. **COMRADES**: This is when two or more competing companies come together to take on a bigger competitor or to augment and consolidate their assets. An example of one such collaboration is KLM and Air France. The leagues of Greece were formed amongst cities that at some point had enmity amongst themselves but rallied together

---

[90] Suk Lee, Bob Song, *Never Give: Jack Ma In His Own Words*,(Agate Publishing 2016)

against a more threatening foe, in the form of the Persians.

    a. In terms of information, share everything relating to the project.
    b. Share information that advances the project and agenda at hand.
    c. Protect trade secrets, patents and business information.

III. **CONFIDANTES**: These are individuals, organisations that have a direct and vested interest in the success of your business because their success is inseparably tied to yours. This relates to key suppliers and customers who determine the survival and growth of your business. Confidantes can know and understand the intimate details of your business and plans. The best example is the relationship between processor chip manufacturers and computer manufacturers; both have to share very detailed technical information about their designs.

SHAPING TECHNOLOGY - SHAPING THE FUTURE

Together with knowledge, technology is of principal importance in the process of developing and maximizing the power of collaboration. Technology implies the way something is done. For example the way in which a message is conveyed can determine the effectiveness of a team.

Though there are differing accounts a story is told of a Greek soldier Phillipides who was sent as a messenger to Athens from the Battle of Marathon to announce the defeat of the Persians. Another account by Herodotus narrates how Phillipides was sent to Sparta to ask for help. In both instances the concept of communicating the message is apparent and clear. The message had to reach its intended recipients and required that a man run a great distance to deliver it. Today, messages are sent right across the world within seconds.

Effectiveness is about doing things well. In the case of Phillipides the communication technology may have been primitive but the principle was the same. The destiny of a nation was hinged on Phillipides' ability to do things well. He had to be a good and fast runner, trustworthy with information and a good communicator. In terms of motivation and morale, technology serves the express purpose of keeping everyone inspired and focused on the end goal. The information Phillipides possessed was critical in both cases to secure the combined alliances with the end goal in sight of keeping the Persians out of Greece.

SPECIALISATION

The Greek city states point to a key aspect that makes collaboration a relevant strategy in the pursuit of business growth. One of the most profound results of these city states was the development of specialisations based on the differences in constitution and interpretation of the constitutional mechanisms. A case in point was the development of the Spartan city state as tactfully expressed in the movie 300.

The success of the Hellenic league in war was largely dependent on Sparta's development and how it specialised in war. The city of Sparta was structured and developed under the strict disciplines and conducts of its army. The economy, social interaction and politics were inseparably linked to its army, serving the purpose of supplying the Greeks specialised resources in the wars against the Persians.[91]

---

[91] P.J. Rhodes, *The Greek City States: A Source Book*, (Cambridge University Press 2007)

To prise market share from a market leader requires specialist skills or unique innovations developed by another company, an individual, supplier or even customer. Leveraging these specialisms can easily serve as a means of creating a competitive advantage.

COLLABORATION FOR GROWTH

> In the practical art of war the best thing of all is to take the enemy's country whole and intact; to shatter it and destroy it is not good at all.[92]

> Sun Tzu

As an army advances and takes more ground it also needs to collaborate with external forces for long term sustainability. For a business to succeed it definitely needs customers. Customers are key stakeholders that determine the success or failure of business. The success of the Greek and Roman empires were initially a result of conquests but were sustained by the communities who were attracted to the Roman or Greek way of life.

---

92 Sun Tzu *The Art of War*

For a business to succeed it needs a group of people keenly interested in the product or service being offered. Initially it may be forced on the customers through aggressive marketing campaigns and so forth but ultimately market share is sustained when customers become willing participants or collaborators in the profitability of the business. This points to the development of a brand.

> Humans do not respond to the physical qualities
> of things but act on what they mean to them.[93]
>
> Krippendorff.

The long term success of a business is down to the experiences customers derive from the product or service. The meaning and experience customers attach to a product or service determines the success of a company much more than great marketing campaigns. It is most profound to hear defeated foes praise the Roman or Greek way of life.

---

[93] Klaus Krippendorff, *The Semantic Turn: A New Foundation Of Design* (CRC Press 2005)

THE GOVERNMENT

"Never, ever do business with government. Love them. Don't marry them. So, we never do projects for government."[94]

Jack Ma

To succeed businesses sometimes need to collaborate with larger stakeholders. Without their support, it can prove difficult to navigate the business environment. Regulators and gate keepers like the government play the express role of ensuring a healthy business environment. Notwithstanding the times that government has supported certain players in the industry whilst stifling the efforts of others; garnering good favour or at least a neutral position is imperative.

THE COMPETITION

So, too it is better to recapture an army entire than to destroy it, to capture it a regiment, a

---

[94] Suk Lee, Bob Song, *Never Give: Jack Ma In His Own Words*

detachment or company entire than to destroy them.[95]

Sun Tzu

In business it is also possible to collaborate with your fiercest competitor. Sometimes this comes by sheer force nonetheless every so often it is the result of having an innovation the competitor needs to advance their business. Presently, in Zimbabwe many banks are forced to partner with other banks to ensure the use of a mobile banking solution. Also when an enemy (competitor) is defeated there is the need to harness their talent, instead of obliterating the competition.

> The captured soldiers should be kindly treated and kept. This is called, using the conquered foe to augment one's own strength.[96]

> Sun Tzu

It is common that the best talent is won by the biggest and best companies who can afford to remunerate their staff well. Yet, sometimes such talent is lured over to smaller

---

[95] Sun Tzu *The Art Of War*
[96] Ibid

businesses, where there is great potential for growth of both the company and employee. The Persians were renowned for a diverse group of fighting soldiers from different nations. This was a result of assimilating those they conquered rather than obliterating them. Assimilation of talent can serve to augment your business and give you the momentum necessary to surge forward.

In history, it has taken strategic alliances to assail and overcome a large and seemingly indomitable force. There are many wars that have been fought where it has taken the support of another partner to ensure victory. In business alliances and partners serve in the same capacity.

They provide a Japanese fisherman the added capacity to breakdown an incumbent's hold on the market. The alliance between the Romans and the Visigoths to repel the Huns in 451 B.C. is an example. The Romans and Visigoths were rarely on civil terms but the threat of the Huns proved a compelling reason to unite.

Collaboration in business comes in many forms; strategic partnerships, key alliances, business-to-business connectivity, supply chain integration, co-opetition, preferred providers, affiliates, joint ventures and so forth. These collaborations show how two forces can come together to attack the dominant incumbent's market share.

In business it is important to know how to parcel out information and knowledge strategically.

I. **AGREEMENTS**: Legal documents, handshakes, brotherhood. Collaboration is built around transparency and integrity. Before sharing critical information it is important to ensure that strategic information and resources are safeguarded by agreements.

II. **LEVERAGING ASSETS**: Collaboration is a means of building an armoury. If we look at the shared economy, what gives companies like UBER and Airbnb an advantage over their incumbent competitors is the fact that they can leverage the assets of their growing community and expand rapidly without expending a lot of capital to build infrastructure.

III. **SHARING KNOWLEDGE**: Shaping ideas and strategy. Cross pollination is critical in the battle for supremacy. The Greek league was able to leverage Sparta's knowledge of the Hot Gates/ Thermopylae to swing the tide of the war.

IV. **SHAPING TECHNOLOGY**: Technology is best shaped within communal spaces. It is a critical determinant in shaping the future. Throughout history technological change was determined both by purposive flows of knowledge upon application of said technology. The *corvus* only improved when it was used in battle. Collaboration is an important determinant of technological advancement and development.

V. **MERGERS, ACQUISITIONS**: Capital raising, resourcing and the dangers thereof. Beyond informal and loose collaborations more strategic marriages can follow that are designed to strengthen the position of the business. This is captured aptly by Sun Tzu, "The captured soldiers should be kindly treated and kept." This is called, using the conquered foe to augment one's own strength. Mergers and acquisitions are designed to augment and enhance the internal strengths of a business much like conquered or treaty soldiers add to the bulwark of a nation. When generals like Hannibal and Alexander the Great conquered territory, they normally strove to preserve the city and would assimilate the resources of the city including its military might.

VI.   **INDUSTRY LEADERSHIP AND INFLUENCE**: It's not size that matters, at times its influence. When small companies hold the industry in balance. Innovation has the potential to give small companies influence in the industry. This is especially the case when you consider the importance of software in certain industries. In Zimbabwe there are many small software companies (comparatively in terms of staff compliment and revenue) that have considerable sway in the banking industry as they supply various forms of software solutions including core banking software.

In a battle for Jerusalem it happened that one of the parties sought the assistance of the Roman army. This collaboration didn't turn out as anticipated after the Romans proceeded to colonize Jerusalem. Collaboration and co-operation have obvious risks therefore it is important to assess the dangers before engaging in one.

SEVEN RISKS OF COLLABORATION

I.   **DIMINISHED MARKET POSITIONING:** Collaboration can always lead to some level of infiltration if your identity is not managed and persevered well through the process. What is of significant importance during and after a collaborative process is to establish whether your competencies have improved and your brand is still visible. The Spartans and Athenians never lost their identity despite being involved in a number of alliances and collaborative excursions. This was down to having strong and well defined competencies, and a distinct and clear brand identity.

II. **INABILITY TO EFFECT SIGNIFICANT CHANGE**: Collaboration also has the potential to diminish power and influence as with the number of people involved in the decision making process and the team dynamics. The Latin phrase *primus inter pares* captures this succinctly.[97] Within any collaborative initiative though there are agreed levels of equality in terms of power, there will always be the first among equals. It is important to be weary of personalities so as to ensure that your influence is neither diminished nor diluted.

III. **PERCEIVED OR REAL REDUCTION IN VALUE:** Collaborations can potentially affect the value that the venture or your enterprise can deliver. The fundamental question comes down to the degree of impact the collaboration is making to the bottom line or end result.

IV. **OPPORTUNITY COST:** Collaborative efforts tend to also require a lot more time and energy.

---

[97] Primus inter pares means first among equals. *Merriam-Webster Dictionary* https://www.merriam-webster.com/dictionary/primus

Collaboration is an investment that can be measured against the prospects of just going at it alone. There is an opportunity cost in pursuing collaborative relationships especially if they end up going awry.

V.   **EXPOSURE TO A WORLDVIEW:** Organisational cultures have a bearing on the quality of execution. Success is inextricably linked to worldview. A degree of pessimism and risk aversion means that an entrepreneur will be cautious in their dealings. As wise as this may seem, it means that over time pessimistic entrepreneurs will miss opportunities for quantum growth. Optimistic entrepreneurs have a worldview that views most things in a positive light and are often risk inclined. Though they are capable of seizing risk, they often end up in difficult circumstances because they did not take the necessary precautions. There are also realistic entrepreneurs who are more aligned to the Stockdale Paradox, "You must retain faith that you will prevail in the end, regardless of the difficulties. And at the same time... You must confront the most brutal facts of your current reality, whatever they might be."[98] Realistic entrepreneurs accept the facts of the present circumstance with a strong dose of hopeful expectation.

VI. **LOSS OF INTELLECTUAL CONTROL**: It is easy to lose control of intellectual property within a collaborative effort if there are no systems in place to manage communication and information.

VII. **DIMINISHED SUPPLIER RELATIONSHIPS**: Supplier relationships are core and often what can happen is that a partner can end up building stronger relationships with your supplier. This means if they become your competitor it will affect your supplier relationship.

---

[98] The *Stockdale Paradox* is the optimism that is most important in becoming a resilient person. https://bigthink.com/think-tank/the-stockdale-paradox-how-optimism-creates-resilience

Chapter 13 SECURITY

The purpose of security is to never permit the enemy to acquire unexpected advantage.[99]

Sgt Maj. Brett Stoneberger

In any given case when a war is fought, a time comes when the attacking force gradually starts gaining ground. This often has positive connotations and boosts the morale of the army as it advances to take on more ground. But there is something important to learn from war.

When it seems the tide is working for you; whatever you have won can easily be lost. Any gains in battle or business should never translate to the enemy or competitor obtaining some benefit. All efforts to grow must be undergirded by efforts to sustain and preserve the advantage.

The concept of Pax Romana and the values engendered therein sustained the Roman Empire for nearly 1500 years. This ideal held the Roman Empire together in spite of the

---

[99] Sgt Maj. Brett Stoneberger, *Combat Leader's Field Guide: 13th Edition*, (Stackpole Books 2005)

numerous insurrections, rebellions, coups and outright anarchy. As Simon Sinek said, "People don't buy what you do; they buy why you do it."[100] Therefore, once market share is gained the important thing is retention. The main focus is to position your business as a pleasurable experience for the customer whatever that may mean.

I. **PROTECT YOUR BUSINESS AND PRODUCT AT ALL COSTS:** It is critical that your positioning within the market place is guarded. This means protecting your brand, products or service. There must never be moments when your product or weaknesses are exposed to allow your competitors to use them against you. Whatever may be deemed a weakness can be converted into strategic actions for defense.

II. **BUILDING STRONG BRAND EQUITY:** Brand Equity points to your business' potential to captivate the minds of your audience consistently and sustainably over the long term. It is not enough to acquire customers it is invariably critical to

---

[100] Simon Sinek, *Start With Why*

retain and then satisfy them. This is one of the most important aspects of security; a long term view of customer needs. This can be calculated and assumed in the customer life time value which focuses on the net profit attributable to the customer over a period. Consider that the expansive Roman Empire had a life span of between 500 and 1500 years, despite so many different challenges and battles. The fundamental question is how long do you want your business to last? If it is trans-generational then building a strong and reputable brand is imperative and subsequently derived from positive and lasting customer experiences.

III. **STICK TO YOUR VALUES:** Values and principles contribute significantly to longevity and security. This is because values are at the core of performance, service delivery and production. Whatever promise we commit to is driven by our ability to fulfill it, which in turn is enshrined in our values.

IV. **CONSOLIDATE MARKET SHARE**: Importantly any gains in the market should be consolidated. Firstly, it is important to reward your team for the success. Rewards come in many different forms but one of the most important is to attribute the victory to those who contributed the most. Secondly, any gains in market share should be supported by a solid branding strategy. It is interesting in certain markets how a brand is associated with an activity and the underlying solution. Just think of how chatting on smartphones is called 'apping' as a reference to the use of Whatsapp. In Zimbabwe mobile money is called Ecocash as a reference to Econet's mobile money service. The most important part of this is how the brand is used to consolidate the hold on the market.

Therefore in chariot fighting, when ten or more chariots have been taken, those should be rewarded who took the first. Our own flags should be substituted for those of the enemy, and the chariots mingled and used in conjunction with ours.

The captured soldiers should be kindly treated and kept. This is called, using the conquered foe to augment one's own strength.[101]

Sun Tzu

In thinking about captured soldiers it's natural to think of talent management. Yet, it can also be considered to be the constituting ingredient of market share. Thus soldiers can be viewed as customers if territory is considered as market share.

Both employees and customers are key ingredients in strengthening an entrepreneur's market position. From the customer's perspective it is a matter of brand loyalty. A market leader exists because he has the loyalty of the customer who defends their position by purchasing the product.

Thus to win over market share an entrepreneur must capture the interest and loyalty of the customer. In the

[101] Sun Tzu, *The Art of War*

most ambitious circumstances an entrepreneur must be positioned to capture the interest and passion of the competitor's best talent. Most importantly customers switch brands because of experience. Continuous bad experiences prime a customer for brand switching whilst a commitment to deliver good experiences ensures that the customer will not switch.

Once the switch happens the customer must associate good experiences with the entrepreneur's brand. Most importantly the success of any campaign is determined by the ability of a general or entrepreneur to advance whilst simultaneously defending what has been won.

One of the most powerful personalities in history is Queen Nzinga of Angola. Her story of resilience and defence stands the test of time and is the cause the Portuguese could not have a permanent foothold in her kingdom, and is worthy of remembrance. In 1623 the Portuguese attacked Queen Nzinga's territory Ndongo, so she fled to another kingdom called Matamba which she conquered and assimilated turning into her capital and secure base. In 1627 she formed a number of alliances with different kingdoms and tribes and led the alliance in a long 30 year war against the Portuguese.[102]

Queen Nzinga was able to secure her position by doing 3 things:

I.   Offering sanctuary to slaves who had run away from the Portuguese.

II.   Accommodating African soldiers trained by the Portuguese in her army.

III. Stirring rebellion amongst the inhabitants of occupied Ndongo.

The Portuguese met with a formidable opponent that they could never defeat and today stands as a lesson in holding a secure position.

Security enhances a business' ability to liberally initiate offensive action by reducing vulnerability to counteraction from a competitor or unanticipated surprise attacks. This is achieved by the entrepreneur's efforts to protect the business and its resources. Security means having clear and active plans of action, an

---

[102] Moses L. Howard, *Nzinga: African Warrior Queen*, (Jugum Press 2016)

awareness of internal human resources and adequate knowledge of a competitor's strategic positioning. It is a matter of managing risk and mitigating the potential pitfalls of offensive market action.

SIX CS OF BUSINESS DEFENCE

You can ensure the safety of your defense if you only hold positions that cannot be attacked.[103]

Sun Tzu

A key trait of a good general is the ability to choose battles wisely, to preserve his energy and the morale of his army. The idea holds true in business when customer acquisition is conducted in such a way as to create an unassailable position in the market.

I. **COMPETENCE**: What you know and how you apply it to business? The Romans were renowned for the close combat skills and also acquired skills in seafaring and building siege works. The Greeks and Macedonians were renowned for their phalanx. Competence is the cornerstone for successful campaigns and enterprise.

---

[103] Sun Tzu, *The Art Of War*

II.   **CONNECTORS AND RELATIONSHIPS:** The networks an entrepreneur creates often determine the business' reach. Relationships are the bedrock of human survival and development. It is not only connections with the end user or customer but the string of networks and relationships necessary to add and deliver value.

III.   **COMPETITIVE ADVANTAGE AND TRADE SECRETS:** Knowledge is a salient aspect of business success. It is a critical component in achieving competitive advantage. This is not merely its acquisition but also its development and enhancement. What has made great brands successful is that ability to generate patentable innovations.

IV.   **CONTAGIOUSNESS:** The network effects of your product that turn initial advantage into Sustainable Competitive Advantage. One of the strongest defence mechanisms is considered to be attack. The degree of 'stickiness' or attractiveness your product has in the eye of the customer is one of the best ways to defend your position.

V.   **COPYRIGHTS AND PATENTS:** Intellectual, human capital and core knowledge within your business needs to be protected through legal machinery such as copyrights, patents, utilities and trademarks. This serves as a rear-guard for any attempts by another business to use the knowledge.

VI. **COMMUNICATION**: Cybernetics is the science of communication and at the crux of it is the concept of feedback. Information and the use thereof is the bedrock of a good defence. Information that comes from the market can represent positive or negative feedback. To develop strong counter strategies it is important to have the right feedback system from the market such as key performance indicators. The core purpose of these indicators is to determine, public opinion, competitor perspectives and customer expectations.

Hence that general is skillful in attack whose opponent does not know what to defend; and he is skillful in defense whose enemy does not know what to attack.[104]

Sun Tzu

Thus growth strategies like niche, value chain reconfiguration and leveraging position an emerging business as a strategic aggressor with an interpretable strategy. The 3 growth strategies present an opportunity to stealthily and tactfully capture market share without drawing too much attention from the competitor. Each

---

Sun Tzu, *The Art of War*

strategy gives the entrepreneur weapons like the *onager* or *corvus*, uniquely suited to the internal competencies of the business. The sign of a good strategy is when an entrepreneur leaves the competitor wondering how the business is advancing and taking market share.

> You may advance and be utterly irresistible if you make for the enemy's weak points; you may retire and be safe from pursuit if your movements are more rapid than those of the enemy.[105]

> Sun Tzu

This is expressly connected to flexible, agile, well defined and maintained strategies. It is difficult for a competitor to prize market share from your business if your strategic plan and approach to the market is hidden from them.

PAX ROMANA AND CUSTOMER SATISFACTION

One of the most profound successes of the Roman Empire was not merely the expansion of the empire through conquest and war but the ability to establish and maintain peace. This peace was called PAX ROMANA or Roman

---

[105] Sun Tzu, *The Art of War*

Peace. For 200 years the Roman Empire was able to establish relative stability over a vast expanse of diverse people groups by establishing an ideology and concept that all people could agree with in the form of law.

Critically for business, acquiring customers is an imperative for establishing a position in the market whilst, customer retention is critical as a springboard for growth. The longevity of the Roman Empire can be attributed to the ability of the emperors to engage in wars but more importantly to establish peace once victory was certain. Without peace all market share gained can easily be lost.

From a business perspective peace points to standards and communication mechanisms tailored to satisfy the customer consistently. Peace also serves as a period to consolidate acquired market share. The peaceful periods during the Roman Empire served as opportunities to build the economy and develop infrastructure. One aspect of defensive strategies is to develop counter measures against competitor retaliation and consolidate growth with the necessary structure and systems.

Build moats

A moat is a ditch, either dry or filled with water, dug around a castle, fortification to create the first line of defence. To preserve and protect any gains in the market there are 5 key moats an entrepreneur can build as a line of defense against retaliation

I.   **Best service**: delivering great service and support to augment the customer offering.

II. **Habit forming**: creating the solution or product that customers will think of when they have a particular need.

III. **Reward program:** create incentives and prizes for customers that are actively engaged in using the products.

IV. **Create stable revenue model:** Revenue models like subscriptions help to build customer loyalty through frequent engagement and create stable cash flows.

V.   **Physical   infrastructure:**   creating   defense mechanisms by building structures around the product that can serve as barriers of entry.

Chapter 14 THE PRINCIPLE OF PURSUIT

Generally speaking the chief aim is the certainty or high probability of victory, that is, the certainty of driving the enemy from the field of battle. The plan of battle must be directed towards this end. For it is easy to change an indecisive victory into a decisive one through the energetic pursuit of the enemy. [106]

Carl Von Clausewitz

The chief aim of business is profitability in all its various forms; financially, psychologically and socially. There is no need to debate the veracity of this, rather to accept that like war, in business someone always occupies the most profitable space in the market. Therefore to achieve profitability an emerging or challenging business must engage in strategies that contend for market share. Yet, in war the aim is not merely to possess a bit of territory but to completely control and influence it for failure to do so

---

[106] Carl von Clausewitz, *Principles of War* 89

would prolong the battle. Hence, entrants to any market must strive to become the market leader.

It is building such a business as to pursue and challenge the existing market leader so as to possess their position of profitability. As Clausewitz says, "For it is easy to change an indecisive victory into a decisive one through the energetic pursuit of the enemy." There is no joy in being considered a market entrant, challenger or substitute for as long as the business is running.

This may reflect a degree of indecision in terms of vision and strategy or even complacency on the part of the entrepreneur. Consider that marketing efforts are by and large owned and determined by the business but branding efforts are expressly and explicitly owned by the customer through derived experience. If this is the case why accept your business' brand as being a secondary option or alternative in the absence of the leading brand in the market? It is critical therefore to pursue a leading and influential market position.

> Our own flags should be substituted for those of the enemy, and the chariots mingled and used in conjunction with ours. [107]
>
> Sun Tzu

Any market share acquired should be branded almost instantly. There is a degree of indoctrination necessary within the game of war and business. The customer should attribute any good experience to your brand and not to the underlying product. If for example the underlying product is sugar the customer should always refer back to your brand as the best experience they have ever derived from sugar. Whenever they think of sugar your brand should come to mind so that when they want to have that experience again they associate it with your brand.

This is how the concept of *Pax Romana* sustained the Roman Empire. The degree of peace and prosperity that was put forward by the Romans delivered an experience that ensured most conquered states and tribes did not see the need for autonomy. The quality of experience, derived value and profit found in being part of the empire

---

[107] Sun Tzu, *The Art of War* 97

far outweighed independence. This must be the case in business. To successfully, attain and maintain a leading position in the market means decisive action and pursuit of creating a brand with a leading presence.

Six Elements of Effective Pursuit of a Competitor

I. **STRONG POSITIONING:** Ensuring that your position is strong enough through customer relationship management. One key element in maintaining and growing market share is developing strong market positioning through effectively meeting customer needs efficiently. It is the sustained pursuit of customer satisfaction no matter how fickle their needs. The key to Roman success in gaining enemy territories was their ability to build strong and positive relationships with the populace.

II. **EFFECTIVE CUSTOMER RETENTION:** Working to retain clientele and grow market share through effective sales, back up and feedback environments. Customer retention is a key ingredient in success and profitability. To be the market leader a business must retain the customer's attention and interest for the longest time and in the most profitable way. For an emerging business to maximize profit it must find comparatively better ways to sell, support and create a pleasurable experience for the customer to the market leader's initiatives.

III. **A MARKET CENTRIC FOCUS:** The greatest danger any business must avoid is to be so inward and product focused as to miss the shifting needs of the customer. For instance in the case of sugar, should the market demand shift to flavoured sugar, businesses that adapt to this need only stand to benefit even more market share. Similarly business that fail to meet these new customer requirements stand to lose their previously acquired markets. Thus a market centric approach, enables a company to positively embrace change especially where customer needs are concerned. The decline of Rome has been attributed to many factors, however the straw that broke the camel's back was the lack of due care with regard to the welfare of the people. When the peoples' needs were ignored the result was agitation and disillusionment which spread over the vast empire. This ultimately led to rebellion and brought the empire to its knees.

IV. **PRODUCT IMPROVEMENT AND DEVELOPMENT:** Continuous improvement is a concept that has driven and shaped the success of most conglomerates in the world. Whatever product development strategies are being applied, customer needs must be converted and packaged within an existing product.

V. **FOCUSED MARKET DEVELOPMENT:** As customer needs evolve so too will market and industry dimensions. Technology has significantly contributed to shifting dimensions in the market giving increasing attention to what are called born global start-ups; companies that grow internationally within 2 years. Modern day technology companies like Netflix, Uber, Amazon and Airbnb do not disrupt their traditional markets by simply driving a technological solution but by creating solutions that meet customer needs.

VI. **CREATING MARKET SPACE USING INNOVATION:** To achieve a larger presence in the market a business must surpass the ambitions of the market leader. Market space means that an entrant to the market can use innovation and initiative to create new frontiers. The Spanish poet Antonio Machado said, "We build the road as we travel." [108] His words embody the notion of pioneering and attempting to go where no other business has gone before. What made the generals that we know in history

---

[108] Ralph Welborn, Vince Kasten, *The Jericho Principle: How Companies Use Strategic Collaboration To Find New Sources Of Value*,(John Wiley & Sons 2003)

famous? They ventured beyond the known confines of that present age. The very notion of a sputnik moment points to attempting the unthinkable and unimagined. If this knowledge captures the attention and interest of the customer it guarantees acquisition and if it is maintained it secures loyalty and retention and most importantly success.

VII. **LEARNING EFFICIENCY:** the competitor is pursued and vanquished by our ability to improve the way an organization learns. The ability to learn is a sure way to improve productivity and reduce the cost of an endeavor. There are five ways to improve learning efficiency:

    a. Labour efficiency
    b. Process Efficiency
    c. Product standardization
    d. Material substitutions
    e. Efficiency in scaling

We should direct our main thrust against an enemy wing by attacking from the front and from the flank, or by turning it completely and attacking it from the rear. Only when we cut off the enemy's line of retreat are we assured of great success in victory.[109]

Carl von Clausewitz

An emerging business entering into the market has different ways it can enter the fray to compete for market share. For survival purposes it must grow and possess the market previously owned by another business, this is at the heart of competitive advantage. Whether the business goes for a full frontal attack, flanking or attacking the rear-guard, the important thing is to block the incumbent's line of retreat and ability to regroup.

The principle of pursuit is designed to ensure certainty of the victory i.e. the territory and market share that has been won. By all intents and purposes the enemy should not be given an opportunity to retreat and regroup as this gives them the chance to try and recover the lost ground.

The strategies at play must scatter and cast the enemy or incumbent into chaos and a distaste for battle. In the case of the great Battle of Thermophylae it is said, the Persian

---

[109] Carl von Clausewitz, *Principles of War*

king lost his taste for battle and retreated back to Persia when he heard of the rousing defeat of his navy.[110] It wasn't enough to push them back it was imperative to exact such a defeat that the Persians lost interest in the territory. This is the same case in business, an entrant must challenge the existing market leader in a specific segment of the market such that the incumbent loses interest in that segment altogether.

> Only when we cut off the enemy's line of retreat are we assured of great success in victory. [111]
>
> Carl von Clausewitz

If we are venturing into business in pursuit of great success and profitability, we must execute our activities like the great generals of old by ensuring that we enter markets for total victory and nothing else will suffice.

> The good fighters of old first put themselves beyond the possibility of defeat, and then waited for an opportunity of defeating the enemy.[112]

---

[110] Terri Doughterty, *300 Heroes: The Battle of Thermopylae*
[111] Carl von Clausewitz, *Principles of War*
[112] Sun Tzu, *The Art of War*

Sun Tzu

One of the great hallmarks of these generals was planning. Before committing resources to advance a product or to enter a market, planning must be the mainstay of all operations. Battles and wars are not often won in the battlefields but in the quiet quarters of a brooding general. The opportunity to win over market share will lend itself to the business that is prepared and positioned to seize it. Above all the ultimate aim of business is not long drawn out tussles for market share but it is to achieve maximum profitability.

> In war, then, let your great object be victory, not
> lengthy campaigns. [113]

Sun Tzu

Lastly, the principle of pursuit is not centred on good marketing efforts because this involves spending money to acquire customers. Rather, it is centred on establishing a strong brand. This may involve marketing campaigns at the very beginning but ultimately a good brand is built

---

[113] Ibid

through delivering great customer experiences. To rephrase Sun Tzu says the object of war and business is not lengthy marketing campaigns but the victories derived from a brand that delivers lasting experiences.

PURSUE MARKET SHARE WITH WISDOM AND IMAGINATION #BUSINESS IS WAR

> "Hannibal, you know how to gain a victory, but not how to use one."[114]
>
> Hannibal's cavalry commander, Maharbal

Importantly pursuit of a competitor requires both strong strategic thinking and wisdom. All efforts in business must be fashioned and designed with wisdom and insight.The saddest narrative in business is always the entrepreneur who created a phenomenal innovation that took the market by storm but failed to gain the necessary traction to create a strong market position. It is one thing to gain the interest of the market and another thing to sustain profitable customer engagement. The reality is that

---

[114] Jann Tibbets, *50 Great Military Leaders of All Time*, (Vij Books India Pvt Ltd 2016)

businesses are no longer competing on data, information or knowledge as these have become ubiquitous. The hallmark of success in business is the ability to repeatedly apply knowledge as well as to create new knowledge sets through imagination and wisdom.

FIVE FRAMES OF THOUGHT.

War and business are built on these five frames of thought. A lack of any of these frames of thought results in some degree of failure or disappointment.

I. **DATA** Statistics and datasets: this consists of any unstructured and structured datasets available concerning the market and existing competitors. It is mostly historical statistical data. Most data is historical in nature and is a reflection of the past or a study and mapping of the past to create conversations and projections of the future. As important as data is it only forms the foundation of good thought and reasoning. There is a paradox to this, it can either say a lot about something and it can also say nothing. To pursue an enemy and competitor on data alone is to pursue them on their past position and former glories.

"The problem with data is that it says a lot, but it also says nothing. 'Big data' is terrific, but it's usually thin. To understand why something is happening, we have to engage in both forensics and guess work. [115]

Sendhil Mullainathan Professor of Economics, Harvard

II.   **INFORMATION** Analysis of past and Interpretation of the past: this is when data is processed and converted to useful information that can be analysed for decision making, necessary for present action. Information is a key ingredient in the process of determining short and medium term direction. The rise and fall of great empires and businesses has been the pervasion of bad

---

[115]

http://www.greatthoughtstreasury.com/author/sendhil-mullainathan

information, misinformation and being uninformed. At the heart of good decision making is the ability to collect and convert data into implementable information. Information changed the course of many battles.

Information is the mortar that both builds and destroys empires.[116]

- Tobsha Learner

III.   **KNOWLEDGE:** Lessons from past and near future for application in the short to medium term: this is information converted to applicable and repeatable experiences that can be delivered consistently. Knowledge points to the acquisition of the necessary skills and competence to shape the future through positive repeated action. Courage on the battlefield wasn't down to fool hardy bravado but to those knowledgeable and skilful enough to fight for survival.

---

[116] James William Fulbright, *The Price of The Empire* (Patheon Books 1989)

A lack of knowledge creates fear. Seeking knowledge creates courage. [117]

George Bernard Shaw

IV. **IMAGINATION** Unbridled visions of the future creative (invariant curiosity and analysis) and synthetic (skill and expert driven analysis): this is a combination of both expert driven analysis of conditions to shape the future and curious and creative explorations of the future using a Periclean lens; shaping the wonderment of ages to come. A rich imagination is the basis for creating viral products and services that transcend geographical borders, impact generations and break cultural boundaries,

Imagination is everything. It is the purview of life's coming attractions. [118]

---

[117]   George Bernard Shaw. *Arms And The Man*,(Courier Corporation 2012)
[118] Perfect Papers, Imagination Is Everything. It Is The Preview Of Life's Coming Attractions: Gold Marble Albert Einstein Quote Inspirational Notebook,(2018)

Albert Einstein

V. **WISDOM**: Practical and long term integrated application of insight: It is an integration of knowledge, imagination, insights and profound understanding. It is a state of thought that embraces uncertainty and ambiguity with fortitude and strength. Importantly it is a level of thinking that is practical and productive in its outcome. Wisdom as Joybell says is not about the number of battles that one fights but about prudent and strategic choice. The long term survival of a business is down to the ability to choose the right battles to fight.

"Choose your battles wisely. After all, life isn't measured by how many times you stood up to fight. It's not winning battles that makes you happy, but it's how many times you turned away and chose to look into a better direction. Life is too short to spend it on warring. Fight only the most important ones, let the rest go." [119]

---

[119] C. Joybell, *The Sun Is Snowing: The Scrapbooks,* (2014)

C. JoyBell

No matter how skilled Hannibal was at war he was never able to win the war and the core reasons are a result of his inability or more critically the Carthaginians inability to convert victories in battle into strategic advantage. The principle of pursuit serves as an important step in the pursuit of competitive advantage.

THREE COMPONENTS OF PURSUING COMPETITIVE ADVANTAGE

1. **BE A TEAM PLAYER:** whether it is with employees, suppliers or customers, success is a shared experience and any excursion into the market should be recognised as a team effort. One of Hannibal's greatest weaknesses was that because he was not a team player the generals and leaders of Carthage, left him to his own devices when he needed their support the most. This is indicative of the dangers of scaling without consideration of the key stakeholders that contribute to your success. It is easy to forget the employee who commits to coming to the office every morning at 8am. Or

neglecting the low cost customer who bought your products the first time.

2. **CONSIDER YOUR SUPPLY LINES AND RESOURCES:** One of the biggest challenges that Hannibal faced was ensuring he had secure supply lines. When he advanced into Italy the best way to receive supplies was via the Carthaginian navy. However the problem was that the Roman navy was at the time much stronger and better equipped. This meant that as Hannibal advanced deeper into enemy territory he was cut off from key supply lines.[120] From a business viewpoint an entrepreneur must manage his growth and scaling strategy. The risk is always to grow too fast without ensuring the business has the necessary resources to maintain a long and competitive onslaught in a competitive market for ultimate victory. It is also imperative never to assume that the competitor is weak and unassuming especially if they are a large corporation. The efforts to grow must be regulated

[120] *Hannibal* *Barca* http://www.livius.org/articles/person/hannibal-3-barca/

by a strong and sober assessment of the competitor.

3. **MANAGE PERCEPTIONS:** It is often stated that perception is reality. Hannibal made an assumption that whilst attacking Italy and Rome he could sway the perceptions of Rome's allies in the surrounding Italian peninsula. Yet, he never anticipated that the surrounding Italian cities had a strongly engrained fear of Rome. How loyal are customers to the opponent's brand? Brand switching is only achievable if customers are not as loyal to a competitor's brand. If the customer's perception of the competitor's brand is strong, then it is very difficult to prise them from it. Therefore to attack and confront a competitor's market share there must be validated evidence that customers are openly ready to switch or that your business has a far superior offering. This validated evidence can be summed up as revenues derived from selling your brand.

Chapter 15 FORMING PUBLIC OPINION

Public opinion is won through great victories and the occupation of the enemy's capital. [121]

Claus von Clausewitz

The best way to build an effective brand is to develop and establish great products that people will love. The legendary leaders and great generals of war were renowned mostly for their great victories, whether it was Caesar, Hannibal, Alexander or Nebuchadnezzar. Success is at the heart of war, so too at the heart of business. One of the best quotes that reflect this in the crudest way possible:

"I am the punishment of God...If you had not committed great sins, God would not have sent a punishment like me upon you." [122]

---

[121] Carl von Clausewitz, *Principles of War*

[122] George Lane, *Genghis Khan and Mongol Rule*,(Hackett Publishing 2009),29

Genghis Khan

When villages and towns heard that Genghis Khan's army was approaching they fled without a fight, not out of strategy like when the Russians fled the Germans in World War 2 but in recognition of Genghis Khan's reputation as a ruthless warrior. The quote reflects Genghis Khan's opinion of himself as well as the reputation he had established with each victory as the punishment of God.

Inversely, it is not the intent in business to be the punishment of God but rather the quote reveals the effects of victory as a basis for being established in the minds of the people. In business it is about establishing and growing market share.

For the entrepreneur the drive should be to be known for a product that is loved and deeply cherished by the customer. It has been said that a company may own the marketing initiative but the customer owns the brand; the customer owns the experience and interaction with the brand.

It is also worthy to note how the swift victory of the Zimbabwean army won over the hearts of the

Zimbabwean people. Following the deployment of troops across the country the army together with a group of civic leaders called for an historic march. It was one of the most momentous occurrences in Zimbabwe's recent history. It points to the importance of victories that shape and form public opinion. To effectively win the war of business, there must be significant, milestones and victories that influence public opinion consistently.

DELIVERING CUSTOMER BASED BRAND VALUE

The origin of the word branding is from the nordic word *brandr* which means to burn.[123] It actually points to etching and engraving a name as a means to identify ownership. Forming public opinion is expressly tied to the value derived by a customer's interaction with the brand.

It is not the physical and material structures of a business that generate profits but the relationships formed with customers and it is brand names that secure them.

---

[123] *Nordic Names* https://www.nordicnames.de/wiki/Brandr

KEY BRAND ELEMENTS

Brand elements: brand name, logo, symbol, character, packaging and promise.

BRAND NAME: The name of a product or business is imperative in the pursuit of deriving customer experiences. The concept of a name is aptly captured in a historical armed cohort of the Persian army called The Immortals.[124]

The name emerged from the nature and way the cohort was replenished and maintained and viewed by the public and surrounding communities as recorded by Herodotus the historian. Hence, creating a brand name is an imperative step in delivering customer experiences that derive value.

LOGO and **SYMBOL:** The Logo is a front facing element of a company and is similar to the standards and guidons of different armies in history. From a military viewpoint standards and guidons served the purpose of identification, honour and distinction. Furthermore, it was

---

[124] http://www.ancient-origins.net/history/immortals-elite-army-persian-empire-never-grew-weak

important to maintain formation by creating a rallying point in the midst of battle.

CHARACTER: Public opinion is derived from the views and perceptions formed by the interaction of the brand with its constituents. In essence character defines association and uniqueness. Character is the distinctive qualities and values that define your brand.

One of the key features of the cohort called Immortals was the perception that they never reduced in number. Whenever an Immortal died or was wounded an apt replacement was conscripted almost instantly. This created the perception of a band of 'immortals' who never diminished in number or stature.

PACKAGING: Ultimately a brand is packaged and presented in the form of a product, service or action. Packaging serves as an important indicator of quality and standards. The Immortals were decked in golden armour which in many ways would have perpetuated their appearance as an immortal fighting force.

PROMISE: Undergirding a brand is a commitment to deliver an experience. The success of a brand is inseparably linked to the commitment and promise made by the creators of the brand. The decline and fall of many armies was often due to internal strife borne out of broken promises. Insurrection, desertion and mutiny are words aptly associated with the disintegration and breakdown of many an army structure. In the case of a business, a broken promise means not meeting the expectations of the customer.

STORYTELLING

A chronicler, scribe or historian was one of the most important people to travel with the army during a war. In many cases they were caught up in battle as observers or participants. Their value was in their ability to record the details in the form of an official document or journal.

We can accredit the records of many historic battles to the exploits and efforts of great writers who were dedicated to the task at hand. A business that stands the test of time needs a lasting and impressionable narrative. A profitable and viable business is a business with a clear and captivating record of its efforts and passions.

I cannot overemphasize the words of Simon Sinek, "People don't buy what you do; they buy why you do it. And what you do simply proves what you believe."[125] All the marketing efforts in the world cannot redeem a faulty brand experience.

What marketing programs and all other communication efforts achieve is validation; proving what the business believes. Genghis Khan was an effective conqueror and the people who encountered him simply confirmed it as a result of the actions derived from his values and beliefs.

LEVERAGE POTENTIAL ASSOCIATIONS

The strength of a good brand is strongly linked to derivative associations. Whether it is associations with the country of origin, a particular emotion, historical events or experiences; a strong brand is often defined by the hierarchy of associations. The Roman Empire will not simply be remembered for its great conquests and battles but also for its opulence, inflation, architectural brilliance, culture, language and innovation.

---

[125] Simon Sinek, *Start With Why*

As much as Pericles was a great general he was also a great orator, philosopher and politician. Great brands are defined by the primary associations and the levels of secondary associations and experiences derived by the customer from inference.

FORMING A MOVEMENT - SETH GODIN

The basis of a strong presence in the market is developing strong ties with key stakeholders, especially customers and building a positive reputation. Seth Godin's ideas around forming a tribe, serve as a solid backdrop to appreciate the importance of a strong narrative and brand.[126] All great armies had a reputation that resulted from gradual and concerted action.

The Roman Empire was originally a motley band of farmers seeking to defend their land but gradually became a great force. The Mongols were successfully transformed from ragged and disorganised bands into marauding

---

[126] Seth Godin, *Tribes: We Need You To Lead Us,* (Little Brown Book Group 2011)

armies under the guidance of Gengis Khan. There are two things we can draw from Seth Godin: [127]

I. "The secret of leadership is simple: Do what you believe in. Paint a picture of the future. Go there. People will follow. The best way to form public opinion is to pursue the objectives and opportunities you believe in passionately

II. The idea that a movement is started by telling a story that creates a connection with people and inspires action. According to Seth Godin, Senator Bill Bradley defines a movement as having three elements:
   a. A narrative that tells a story about who we are and the future we are trying to build.
   b. A connection between and among the leader and the tribe.
   c. Something to do - the fewer the limits the better. Any action that is required must be simple to execute with very few impediments or obstacles.

In the unification process of the Mongols, Genghis Khan had allies and soldiers from different religious backgrounds

---

[127] Ibid

under his leadership. Though he was an animist, he had Christians, Muslims and Buddhists under his leadership.

This highlights the importance of leadership, that though your subordinates and partners may be from divergent belief and value systems it is possible to unite them under one common goal in pursuit of success. Furthermore, painting the right narrative of a desired future creates the right connection to build the army necessary to take on the market.

FINDING AND UNCOVERING THE REMARKABLE

The deepest treasure, is the lasting impression an experience or encounter with your brand makes on your customer. The words of Pericles ring true, "Future ages will wonder at us as present ages wonder at us now." The Greek society and their approach to politics, economics and war are deeply entrenched within our society in the present age.

The wonderment we draw from the Greeks is derived from their ability and passion to go out in pursuit of remarkable experiences. One of the greatest leaders and generals,

Alexander the Great spread Greek ideologies as far afield as India. How far will your brand extend? It is all dependent on how you shape public opinion.

SHARE OF VOICE AND SHARE OF MIND

What you say and what people think about and whether they recall what you say.

SHARE OF VOICE: It will not always be the loudest brands that will be heard but the clearest and most poignant communicators of value. In the midst of the noise and clutter of war the effectiveness of the, cavalry men, snipers, ninja and assassins need to be acknowledged. What the public knows and appreciates is the success of war and the heroes that are presented before them.

The victories and legends of bygone eras were sometimes shaped by the exploits of lone operators whose actions turned the tide of a battle and changed the course of a war. The idea of having a share of the voice is to ensure that your business' story is told.

Often it is said that history is told from the perspective of the victor. But one of the most profound narratives of history is the resilience of the Japanese people after Hiroshima and Nagasaki.

Instead of being totally vanquished and using this disastrous point in their history as an excuse Japan has emerged as one of the most powerful economies in the world. Their story is not of defeat but resilience and hope against the odds.

SHARE OF MIND: Do the customers think of you when they need a specific service? A story is told of how Jerusalem came to be conquered by the Romans. The story goes that there was a power struggle between two brothers Hyracanus and Aristobolus who both enlisted the aid of Pompey to resolve the dispute.

The profound part of this is that both brothers sought to resolve the issue by negotiating with the army they thought was most powerful.[128] Do your customers think of your brand as the most powerful, effective or reliable? Is your brand positioned in the mind of your customer as the go to brand?

---

[128] Fendel, *Chanuka: Season Of Valour,* (Feldheim Publishers)

THE FIVE POWERS OF FORMING PUBLIC OPINIONS IN BUSINESS

I. **POWER OF MEMORY**: Can your brand be remembered easily? What makes Genghis Khan's quote so poignant was that he was genuinely considered the punishment of God based on how he went about conquering states. More importantly it was the memory imprinted on the minds of those who survived his attacks because they are the people who told his story. Everyone including your competitor can be your most reliable and enabled story teller. Your marketing initiatives create the points of contact and your business can determine the degree and level of contact but ultimately the derived experience belongs to the customer and all others who interact with your brand. No matter how many chroniclers Genghis Khan had, his best story tellers would have been the people who called him a marauder, barbarian and so forth because they had the experience to show for it.

II. **POWER OF MEANING**: Is it rich in visual and verbal imagery? The greatest brands in history are remembered for the ability to generate meaning. It is not in the vainglorious pursuits of success that legends are born but when generals and entrepreneurs endeavor to pursue purpose and meaning. Does it have credibility or can you build credibility? What does it mean? Are the experiences your customers and competitors derive valid and meaningful? There are 3 things that engender experience in customers namely, the messenger, the way the message is conveyed and the validity and veracity of the message.

III.   **POWER OF TRANSFER**: Can it move within and across boundaries (product categories, geographic, cultural, language etc.)? In ancient times language was one of the greatest barriers to conquest and advancement. Yet, it is profound to note the presence of Greek and Latin across the known world. This points to the transferable power of viral ideas. Viral networks were not created by modern social media frameworks like Facebook but by ideas and brands that transcended boundaries. Greek ideas of rule and governance, the concept of Roman peace were all viral in their nature over centuries. What social media frameworks did was change the speed of dissemination. Therefore an important ingredient in the spread of a brand is its ability to be transferred into different contexts. Viral business ideas are multi-dimensional in that they will do 4 things

○   **HORIZONTAL:** They will travel around the globe, from one geographical area to another.

- VERTICAL: They will diffuse into cultures through different classes of people.
- TEMPORAL: They will consistently be passed on to future generations.
- ETERNAL: They will impact eternity.

IV. **POWER OF ADAPTATION**: flexibility and ease of response to changing times. The hallmark of Roman cavalries and infantries was their ability to shift and change as situations arose during battle. This shaped their reputation as a conquering force. Conquest is hinged on the ability to embrace change and to adapt to changing conditions appropriately. Great nations were established and sustained by their ability to adapt to shifting conditions. The rapidity and volatility of our times make adaptation an imperative in business success.

V. **POWER OF SECURITY**: Public opinion is drawn from trust and guarantees of sustainability. Security is a matter of establishing how easily an entrepreneur's position can be defended and sustained over a period of time. This can be done through a legal process which can be referred to as rules of engagement or through competitive security. One of the most profound imageries in war of security was the view of walled cities. Once a territory was conquered and secured, the next phase was to build the defensive walls.

THE ROAD LESS TRAVELLED

> Traveller there is no path. The path must be forged by walking. [129]
>
> Antonio Machado

The great wars were won by an ardent pursuit of victory and often the generals who won them chose to make paths themselves. People rally and surround the adventurer and innovator because they want to be associated with potential greatness. To be successful in business requires the entrepreneur to choose the path not well worn.

Public opinion is influenced by great victories and successes undergirded by strong branding. There is no road to success based on the well-worn paths of your predecessors, rather the new path must be forged by pursuit of building a lasting brand.

---

[129] Antonio Machado, *There Is No Road*, (White Pine Press 2003)

Well-worn paths serve as points of reference and wisdom but cannot replace the entrepreneur's decision to pursue a particular vision with the right strategy.

> "The real test of a man is not when he plays the role that he wants for himself but when he plays the role destiny has for him."[130]

> Vaclav Havel

The destiny of great men and women was and is shaped by larger than life visions so too the destiny of great businesses. Pericles once said, "Where the rewards of valour are the greatest, there you will also find the best and the bravest spirits among the people."[131] The world en masse will give way to the businesses and ideas with visions that transcend the mundane and ordinary to deliver lasting value.

---

[130] Christina Abby, *Flippin' The Script*,(FriesenPress 2013)
[131] Jasper Neel, *Aristotles's Voice : Rhetoric, Theory and Writing in America*,(SIU Press, 1994)

POST WAR

Chapter 16 YOUR SPUTNIK MOMENT

It takes presence of mind to appreciate that not having first mover advantage does not end your pursuit of success. You may not be the first in space but you will surely not be considered insignificant.

You have the capacity to take on a strong incumbent because you have a set of principles that guide your growth path towards a quantum leap. The 13 principles of war in business highlighted in this book are a means and way to achieve the desired success and growth.

Sun Tzu says, "We may know that there are five essentials for victory:

I. **"He will win who knows when to fight and when not to fight."** Use these 13 principles to choose your battles wisely and to invest in building a strong business.

II. **"He will win who knows how to handle both superior and inferior forces."** Learn to work with minimal resources as a master *strategoi*. Some of the greatest generals in history worked with inferior forces to attain victory making use of strategy.

III. **"He will win whose army is animated by the same spirit throughout all its ranks."** The power of motivation and inspiration.

IV. **"He will win who, prepared himself, waits to take the enemy unprepared."** The 13 principles help your business prepare to take on your competitor by unlocking your unique abilities

V. **"He will win who has military capacity and is not interfered with by the sovereign."** Leadership that does not hinder the organic growth of the business

The 13 principles laid out in this book will help to give your business the right momentum to harness your sputnik moment. They will ensure that you acquire the right levels of wisdom and knowledge to time your entry into the market, when to launch a product, the strategies and tactics necessary to counter the efforts of their competitor and importantly the sweet taste of victory. Nothing more is imperative than having the necessary tools to win market share.

Hence the saying: If you know the enemy and know yourself, you need not fear the result of a hundred battles.[132]

Sun Tzu

Whatever we fear most in business is often a result of ignorance and gross unpreparedness. By implementing the principles laid out in this book you will come to know yourself and know the enemy, thereby guaranteeing a victorious outcome in the marketplace. Finally in summary, to grow and survive entrepreneurs need the following:

I. **A Secure Base:** Position your business to launch a victorious campaign.

II. **Strategic Thinking:** Think like a general preparing for war.

III. **Visioning and Goal Setting:** Pursue what you see. The great tomorrows are bestowed to those that see them.

---

132 Sun Tzu, *The Art Of War*

IV. **Sustaining the Vision and Goal:** Develop the necessary structures and culture to pursue the vision.

V. **Initiating Offensive Action:** Attack without hesitation or delay.

VI. **Concentration of Forces:** Focus on strategic targets where you can maximise success.

VII. **Economy of Forces:** Clearly determine and count the cost of any action.

VIII. **Stealth Attacks:** Attack when it will guarantee you maximum success.

IX. **Mobility and Flexibility (effective and efficient decision making):** Move swiftly and intently.

X. **The Power of Cooperation (power of team and collaboration):** Find people to work with.

XI. **Security (protecting secured positions and markets):** Defend what you win.

XII. **The Principle of Pursuit (going for it):** Pursue until victory is guaranteed.

XIII. **Forming Public Opinion (building brand equity):** Build a lasting brand.

It is not the strongest or the most intelligent who will survive but those who can best manage change.[133]

Leon C. Megginson

Applying these 13 principles will certainly change the fortunes of your business. As Leon Megginson says, survival is really down to how best we manage the only inevitability in life; change.

Finally, every entrepreneur should aim for the 3 results of good execution aptly summarized as **CAR**:

i.   **Complete Thoughts:** developing a concept to its logical end. Half-baked ideas lead to half baked-baked actions and ultimately half-baked results.

ii. **Accomplished Objects:** Goals that are not only achievable but more importantly achieved. Let action and effort be so endowed in an entrepreneur that results are visible and revealed by sustainable profits.

[133] Abhishek Kumar, *The Richest Engineer: A Story That Will Unravel The Secrets Of The Rich,*(Manjul Publishing 2017)

iii.   **Realized Vision**: Ultimately, the intent or design of any activity is to be fulfilled in the pursuit of a great vision. Nothing is more satisfying than to see a dream realized and lived.

#businessiswar so fight for survival, growth and importantly profitability.

Bibliography

Abby, Christina. Flippin' The Script, Friesen Press 2013.

Alpern, Stanley B. Amazons of Black Sparta: The Women Warriors of Dahomey, NYU Press 2011

Billows, Richard A. Kings and Colonists: Aspects of Macedonian Imperialism, Brill 1995.

Black Belt Magazine, August 1968.

Boudicca's Rebellion AD 60–61: The Britons rise up against Rome

Carey, Brian Todd; Allfree, Joshua; Cairns, John. Warfare In The Ancient World, Pen and Sword.

Cartledge, Paula. Spartan Reflections, University of California Press 2003.

Clark, Dan. The Art of Significance, Penguin Publishing Group 2013.

Coker, Linda D. Larentina: Myth, Legend, Legacy Universe 2011.

Collins, Jim. Good To Great: Why Some Companies Make The Leap And Others Don't, HarperCollins 2001.

Doughterty, Terri. 300 Heroes: The Battle of Thermopylae, Capstone 2009.

Fendel. Chanuka: Season of Valour, Feldheim Publishers

Flinn, Steven Optimising Data-To-Learning-To-Action: The Modern Approach To Continuous Performance Improvement for Business, Apress 2018.

Frankl, Victor E. Man's Search for Meaning, Beacon Press 2006.

Fulbright, James William. The Price of Empire, Patheon Books 1989.

Galloway Dale E. Confidence without Conceit, F.H. Revell, 1989.

Giles. Sun Tzu On The Art Of War, Routledge 2005.

Godin, Seth. Tribes: We Need You To Lead Us, Little Brown Book Group 2011.

Green, D.H. Language and History In The Early Germanic World, Cambridge University Press 2000

Greene, Robert. The 33 Strategies of War, Profile Books 2010.

Grossman, Mark. World Military Leaders: A Bibliographical Dictionary, Infobase Publishing 2007

Handy, Charles. The Age of Unreason, Random House 2012.

Howard, Moses L. Nzinga: African Warrior Queen, Jugum Press 20.

Jones, Alonzo T. The Great Empires of Prophecy: From Babylon To The Fall Of Rome, Teach Services Incorporated 2014

Karami, Azhdar. Strategy Formulation in Entrepreneurial Firms, Ashgate Publishing Ltd 2007.

Kumar, Abhishek. The Richest Engineer: A Story That Will Unravel The Secrets Of The Rich, Manjul Publishing 2017

Lane, George. Genghis Khan and Mongol Rule, Hackett Publishing 2009.

Machado, Antonio. There Is No Road, White Pine Press 2003.

Malik, F., 2016. Strategy: Navigating the Complexity of the New World (Vol. 3). Campus Verlag

Mason, John. Believe You Can, The Power of A Positive Attitude, Revell 2010.

Mineo, Bernard. A Companion To Livy, John Wiley & Sons 2014.

Neel, Jasper. Aristotle's Voice: Rhetoric, Theory and Writing in America, SIU Press 1994.

O'Neill, Geri. Make The Best Of The Rest Of Your Life, DoctorZed Publishing 2010.

Perfect Papers. Imagination Is Everything. It Is The Preview Of Life's Coming Attractions: Gold Marble Albert Einstein Quote Inspirational Notebook, 2018.

Peters, Tom. Thriving On Chaos: Handbook for a Management Revolution, HarperCollins 1988.

Ralph Welborn, Vince Kasten. The Jericho Principle: How Companies Use Strategic Collaboration To Find New Sources Of Value,John Wiley & Sons 2003.

Reeves, Martin. Your Strategy Needs A Strategy: How To Choose And Execute The Best Approach, Harvard Business Review Press.

Rhodes, P.J. The Greek City States: A Source Book, Cambridge University Press 2007.

Samuriwo, Musekiwa. The Shark and the Japanese Fisherman, African Knight 2013.

Shaw, George Bernard. Arms and the Man, Courier Corporation 2012.

Sinek, Simon. Start with Why, Portfolio/Penguin 2011.

Slywotzky, Adrian. The Profit Zone: How Strategic Business Design Will Lead you To tomorrow's Profits, Crown Publishing Group, 2007.

The Bible. Authorized King James Version, Oxford UP, 1998.

Tibbets, Jann. 50 Great Military Leaders of All Time, Vij Books India Pvt Ltd 2016.

Tolkien, John Ronald Reuel. The Lord Of The Rings: Volume One, Houghton Mifflin Harcourt 2012.

Tse-tung, Mao. On Guerilla Warfare, Courier Corporation 2012.

Tzu, Sun the Art of War, Cosimo Inc 2010.

Von Clausewitz, Carl. On War - Completed: Great Essays, 2016.

Von Clausewitz, Carl. Principles of War, Courier Corporation 2012.

Welby, Derek A. The Kingdom of Kush: The Naptan and Meroitic Empires, British Musuem Press 2002.

Young, Melanie. Follow Your Dreams, Lulu.com 2013.

Zartman, Sharkie. Shark Sense: Getting In Touch With Your Inner Shark, iUniverse 2011

http://afrikanknight.blogspot.com/2012/10/imaginationis-more-important-than.html

http://www.britannica.com

https://www.facebook.com/strivemasiyiwa/photos/learn-to-find-the-game-changer-part-1

http://www.bridgeguys.com/sec/poems/collection/TheNig htTheyBurnedShanghai.html

https://en.wikipedia.org/wiki/Combat_endurance

https://en.wikipedia.org/wiki/M-Pesa

Hannibal Barca
http://www.livius.org/articles/person/hannibal-3-barca

https://bigthink.com/think-tank/the-stockdale-paradox-how-optimism-creates-resilience

http://www.greatthoughtstreasury.com/author/sendhil-mullainathan

https://www.nordicnames.de/wiki/Brandr

http://www.ancient-origins.net/history/immortals-elite-army-persian-empire-never-grew-weak